D0501167

CALGARY PUBLIC LIBRARY

APR - - 2011

GREEK REVIVAL

Herbed Lamb Parcels, p. 152

GREEK REVIVAL

COOKING FOR LIFE

Patricia Moore-Pastides

Foreword by Dimitrios Trichopoulos

With Photographs by Keith McGraw

The University of South Carolina Press

© 2010 University of South Carolina

Published by the University of South Carolina Press
Columbia, South Carolina 29208

www.sc.edu/uscpress

Manufactured in China

19 18 17 16 15 14 13 12 11   10 9 8 7 6 5 4 3 2

LIBRARY OF CONGRESS CATALOGING-IN-PUBLICATION DATA

Moore-Pastides, Patricia.
  Greek revival: cooking for life / Patricia Moore-Pastides; foreword
by Dimitrios Trichopoulos.
    p. cm.
  Includes bibliographical references and index.
  ISBN 978-1-57003-939-3 (cloth : alk. paper)
  1. Cookery, Greek. 2. Nutrition—Greece. 3. Diet—Greece. 1. Title.

  TX723.5.G8M67 2010
  641.59495—DC22   2010008270

In gratitude to my husband, Harris, and to our parents:

Jean Coleman Moore, John Francis Moore, Anastasia Theodoulou Pastides, and Andreas Pastides. Their loving hands prepared a lifetime of meals, and their hearts created homes that were filled with dreams for us.

Yogurt Parfaits with Blueberries and Lemon Curd, p. 198

CONTENTS

FOREWORD

When Patricia Moore-Pastides asked me whether I would be willing to write a foreword for her *Greek Revival: Cooking for Life,* I did not hesitate—even though I had not, at the time, read the book. After all, I knew from her previous work and our long acquaintance that she is a talented writer, a person of sharp intellect and, more important, sensitivity and compulsion to perfection. I also felt reasonably qualified in spite of my very limited expertise in cooking. I have lived for more than forty-five years in Greece, a cradle of the traditional Mediterranean diet (and another twenty-five in the multiethnic United States, allowing for a sound control group in culinary experiences). I am also an epidemiologist, serving the discipline that documented the beneficial health effects of the traditional Mediterranean diet. Finally I have been

A door in Crete. Photograph by Harris Pastides

married for more than forty years to Antonia Trichopoulou, who has contributed more than any other scientist, save the legendary Ancel Keys, to the revival of the Mediterranean diet and the demonstration of its amazing health advantages. We Greeks are deeply convinced that the traditional Greek diet is the "real prototype" of the Mediterranean diet, although our neighbors in the olive-tree-growing areas of the Mediterranean, including Italians and Spaniards, think otherwise—perhaps with equal justification.

When I actually read the manuscript and found that it was even better than I thought it would be, I was faced with a problem. How can I assure the readers that I did not have a conflict of interest in my assessment of the book? These days, you cannot submit a paper for publication without assuring the editor of the journal that you do not have such a conflict. Read these few sentences from Patricia's book to realize why the Greek diet is inherently superior to "artificial" diets developed on the basis of findings from scientific research, which impose restrictions on various foods, or categories of foods, or nutrients. And keep in mind that until the late 1960s, when adult Greeks kept to their traditional diet, they also had the longest life expectancy in the world, notwithstanding their miserable smoking habits and a health-care system that leaves much to be desired: "Greeks do not *traditionally* eliminate foods from their diet. Because of the emphasis on plant-based foods, food is not weighed or measured. . . . Because mainly healthful fats are eaten, grams of fat are not calculated. Because whole grains are consumed, carbohydrates are not shunned. How freeing it is that by following traditional food choices and patterns, eating does not have to be analyzed, but can simply be enjoyed." In my forty-year professional life in epidemiology, including nutritional epidemiology, I have never heard or read such a concise statement highlighting the advantages of the Greek diet, as it used to be when I was a child or a young man.

Science has documented that the traditional Greek diet is as health promoting as it is delicious. And Patricia's book provides wonderful avenues to this diet through a collection of masterful recipes.

Patricia draws a parallel between the revival of classical Greek architecture in the United States at the beginning of the nineteenth century and the current revival of the traditional Greek diet. Culture has many dimensions, and different people rank them in different ways. Patricia's book honors a particular aspect of Greek culture and, just as important, provides a blueprint for cooking for life—a longer, healthier, and more enjoyable life.

Dimitrios Trichopoulos

PREFACE

There was an additional factor which particularly distinguished the Greeks from their neighbours, namely the extent to which they represented these forms of eating in poetry and literature from Homer through to late antiquity. In two different cities, Syracuse and Athens, they developed the dramatic form of comedy in whose discourse food was a major element.

JOHN WILKINS, *The Boastful Chef:*
The Discourse of Food in Ancient Greek Comedy

Greeks eat like there's no tomorrow and build houses like they'll live forever.

COUSIN DINO, Larnanca, Cyprus, July 2006

Food has always been important in Greek culture. My interest in Greek food, and subsequently in writing this book, began when I married into a Greek family. My husband was the first to be born in America. Even his sister was born in Cyprus. When we were first married, his parents' initial question on the phone never varied: "What are you cooking for dinner?" All the family events celebrated with his family were unique to me, and the new foods quickly became palatable.

Coriander, garlic, and lemon turned green olives, something I'd never liked, into something I craved. Rock-hard green olives soaked in a giant Ball jar for weeks on my in-laws' kitchen counter. The family was impatient for their debut on the table. Of course in Queens, my mother-in-law didn't pick them herself but purchased unripened olives in her Astoria neighborhood market.

And she hammered potatoes. Yes, with a carpenter's hammer! How else could she create multiple surfaces to fry up golden brown and so crispy? Her homemade sausages were draped across an old stickball bat between two

Architectural treasures
with dandelion greens.
Photograph by Harris
Pastides

kitchen chairs to dry. The Easter rolls were filled with a salty cheese and sweet golden raisins, a curious combination. Food was certainly central in the Greek American family, and there was a lot in the cuisine to pique my interest.

In 1988 my husband and I spent ten months in Athens on sabbatical. Since I wasn't working there, I enrolled in Greek-language lessons and joined a gym. There I found a sign in English advertising cooking classes. The instructor was a Greek American woman who had married and relocated to Athens. Her father-in-law owned a *taverna*. *Tavernas* are restaurants that serve a host of authentic Greek dishes and nothing else. Their menus are essentially all the same, with nuanced versions of standard fare. They are found everywhere—cities, countryside, and seaside. A good *taverna* will have a following. It will be packed with patrons on Sunday afternoons. In nice weather they sit outdoors at paper-draped tables under shade trees shared with hungry cats. When the weather is inclement, diners sit shoulder to shoulder indoors at long tables with straw-seat chairs squeezed tightly together. *Tavernas* are the source of long-tried and perfected recipes. Not a bad way to get one's start in Greek cooking.

My class comprised three women from Japan and me. When it came to the *spanakopita* recipe, their origami experience gave them a distinct advantage. Their triangular *pitas* were perfect—tightly folded and of uniform size—while mine were, well, irregular. We shared a great introduction to preparing Greek cuisine. We squeezed endless water from spinach with our hands, strained yogurt through cheesecloth, smashed garlic, grated tomatoes, pureed fish roe, and "debeaked" squid. Best of all we brought our creations home, and mine were received encouragingly.

Reinforcement for this new interest came when we returned from our sabbatical and hosted a Greek party for our neighbors. Our friends were delighted with the menu: *spanakopita, tiropita, tzatziki, salata horiatiki, moussaka, baklava,* and even chocolate *baklava* (evidence of having had a Greek *American* instructor). From that day forward, whatever the party, I was asked to bring "anything Greek."

Recently we spent three months in Cyprus, where we experienced some new dishes and flavors with a Middle Eastern flair. There I was able to spend time testing recipes and assessing the differences between Athenian culinary traditions and those of the island of Cyprus.

The traditional foods of the Mediterranean are delicious and, for that reason alone, should be shared. But my intention in writing about and teaching Greek cooking goes deeper than taste. After thirty years in public health, I firmly believe that we can arrest obesity, diabetes, heart disease, cancer, and Alzheimer's disease by leading more healthful lives. We all face genetic and/or environmental risk factors that are not within our control, but there are many risk factors we can control through how we live. Daily exercise, eating a traditional Greek diet, and choosing not to smoke are the ones to which I subscribe. The health information provided here is not intended to supplant any treatments that may have been prescribed by your physician, and it's a good idea to consult your doctor before making lifestyle changes. The good news is that, with a Mediterranean diet, you can love to eat, feel great, and not feel the least bit deprived!

I hope you will enjoy preparing these recipes. Remember to take your time, take pleasure in the process, and prepare them with love. These steps will assure a delectable meal that you and your family and friends will enjoy, taking time to savor the food, wine, good conversation, and most important, each other. Καλή όρεξη *(Kali órexi)!* Or as the French would say, *bon appetit!*

On the way to the birthplace of Aphrodite, Cyprus. Photograph by Harris Pastides

ACKNOWLEDGMENTS

My sincere appreciation to all who helped with this project, especially the students of Columbia's Cooking! who were the first to cook and often to edit the recipes. Since there is no faster way to lose one's love of cooking than by writing a cookbook, your excitement kept me motivated.

And moving from inception to publication I would like to personally thank the following individuals:

Harris Pastides for wanting a home on a Greek island, for encouraging me to think big, and for not complaining (excessively) when my recipes weren't the same as his mom's;

Katharine Pastides for being a "healthy foodie," for cooking great food with love, and for curing ten pounds of olives just like Yia Yia's;

Andrew Pastides for making a slapdash summer-squash recipe into a keeper and for loving me despite my persistent "eat more vegetables" message;

Barbara DeLaurentis for deciphering stacks of curled-up yellowed papers with cryptic notes to share the secrets of the splendid Pastides cuisine;

Marjorie Spruill for insisting that I come visit the Schlesinger Library at Harvard University, then letting me stay several days so I could conduct research there, and most especially for coming up with a title that stuck;

Jane Teas, my "internet search engine" incarnate, for keeping me up-to-date on the latest studies of the Mediterranean diet;

James Hébert for inviting me to cook with Columbia's Cooking! of the University of South Carolina Cancer Prevention and Control Program, for editing the nutrition information in *Greek Revival,* and for being the consummate composter;

Susan Steck for editing the nutrition information in *Greek Revival;*

Brook Harmon and Brooke Roper for bringing healthy cooking to Columbia;

Fred Drafts for taking the bold step of growing organic vegetables in the President's House garden, which was a gift to me. Fred passed from this life on May 21, 2010. With his passing my colleagues and I lost a brother, a friend, and a mentor.

It is with the joy of Fred's memory that I thank Kevin Woods, Joe Mikolai, and Ginger Adams, who continue to expertly cultivate the magnificent gardens he left us. Their flowers and vegetables will forever grace our President's House events.

I would also like to thank:

Pat Callahan and Brandi Lariscy-Avant for providing expert art direction and an awesome dish collection;

Keith McGraw and Phil Sawyer for taking sixteen hundred photographs and then just one more—and for Keith's two-day marathon slide show, which made it possible to hone;

Pam Bowman for using more moves than the women's volleyball team to protect my time so I could stay on task;

Tom McNally for offering me a private space to work in the Thomas Cooper Library, a place where no one could find me;

Lisa Robinette for keeping my pantry stocked with ingredients for photo shoots when I was cooking ten to twelve recipes per day and for her inexhaustible dedication to making everything easier and prettier;

Bob Moore for his "grilling the perfect tuna" advice;

Marcia Montgomery for the beautiful pottery featured on the dust jacket;

James Ellison for grilling and styling with a true chef's eye;

Catherine Catalano, Cassie Hrushesky, and Pamela Monette for being sous chefs and dishwashers extraordinaire on photo-shoot days;

Betsy Suddeth, Debbie Kassianos, and Michelle Lockhart for providing technical support for my limited computer skills;

Ero Aggelopoulou Amiridis for picking up where my meager Greek left off in translating recipe titles;

Karen Rood, my project editor, for reading with care and delivering order and clarity to this work;

Last but not least, Curtis Clark, director of the University of South Carolina Press, for being a man of few words and fewer e-mails but good advice, a most welcome style!

INTRODUCTION

Greek Revival architecture, which became popular in the United States at the beginning of the nineteenth century, remains a majestic and timeless classical building style. Large fluted columns, scrolling capitals, colonnades, porticos, and friezes characterize this architecture. As American architect Asher Benjamin wrote in 1830, "The three essential and distinct qualities in [Greek] architecture are *strength, grace and richness*" (Benjamin, *The Practical House Carpenter,* III). Such architectural qualities were employed in the design of our federal and state buildings, including the Capitol, the White House, and many state capitols. Reminiscent of the ancient temples of Greece, this architectural style is both visually magnificent and evocative of democracy. Thomas Jefferson, Benjamin Henry Latrobe, and James Hoban all contributed to the Greek Revival movement in the United States. Learning from them, architects such as Robert Mills followed. In addition to the Washington Monument, he designed sixteen neoclassical county courthouses across the state of South Carolina as well as other state and federal buildings. As Mills intended, these imposing and serious stately structures inspire national pride (Edgar, ed., *The South Carolina Encyclopedia,* 637–38). They channel the spirit of democracy itself. "People rule" in a *demokratia,* a system of government where every voice is heard.

Just as the presence of Greek Revival architecture has the power to evoke the very seed of our political ideology, *Greek Revival: Cooking for Life* can empower our long and healthy lives by reviving ancient food traditions. These traditions include cooking and eating from the bounty of nature while taking the time to truly enjoy what matters.

In *Greek Revival: Cooking for Life,* we look back and embrace the so-called peasant diet, which was in fact opulent—resplendent with colorful seasonal vegetables and fruits; seafood; whole grains, nuts, and seeds made into dense breads; meat only on holy days; and legumes to provide protein during most other times.

"Let food be your medicine."
(Hippocrates, 460–337 B.C.E.)

"Let us not drink and eat
everything merely to satisfy
the belly." (Athenaeus,
200 C.E.)

Central to it all was—and still is—olive oil. The source of rich, satisfying flavor and the gift of Athena to the world, olive oil was thought to hold life-giving properties. It was used heavily for cooking, medicinal purposes, and religious celebrations, and it was the prize for victors at the Olympic games (Knickerbocker, *Olive Oil,* 6). Today its salubrious qualities are well accepted, and we view it as nature's gold.

With *Greek Revival: Cooking for Life,* we have a new Greek Revival that holds the power to overcome the health challenges we face today. Here you will find simple, luscious, fragrant, colorful, and healthful recipes but not a diet regime. You will read stories of life in Greece and Cyprus demonstrating a lifestyle that is both simple and sumptuous. You will read about the health benefits of foods, but you won't count calories or grams of fat. You will eat the bread! At the end of a meal, you may just find yourself peeling oranges and passing the sweetest, most succulent slices to your guests.

Greek Revival: Cooking for Life is a recipe for reinvigorating our bodies and reviving our spirits. Through it we embrace the opportunity to be healthy because it's so sensually satisfying to do so. The food is delicious, and the time for savoring is ours to own.

STUDYING THE TRADITIONAL MEDITERRANEAN DIET

We are fortunate today to have results from a half century of research into the Greek diet and lifestyle. This research has identified numerous health

A stylized column made of Parian marble. Photograph by Harris Pastides

benefits associated with this way of life. Overall longevity and reduced risk of heart disease, stroke, cancers, diabetes, Alzheimer's disease, age-related blindness, arthritis, birth defects, asthma and allergies have been attributed to the traditional Greek diet and lifestyle.

As early as 1958, Ancel Keys, an American physiologist, recognized that the men of the island of Crete lived long, full, active lives. Keys was the first to document the diet and lifestyle and to coin the term "Mediterranean diet." His central findings were that the men of Crete lived longer because of their simple diet, which consisted of olive oil, grains (mostly breads), beans, vegetables, and fruit with smaller quantities of animal products.

Keys's "Seven Countries Health Study" compared the men of Crete with those from six other countries and followed them over many years. Compared to Americans, the men of Crete had half the cancer death rate and one twentieth the coronary artery disease of American men (Simopoulos and Robinson, *The Omega Diet*).

Years of nutrition research at Harvard University were summarized in Dr. Walter Willett's book *Eat, Drink, and Be Healthy,* in which he designed the Healthy Eating Pyramid to incorporate the recommendations of current nutritional research. As in the traditional Greek diet, his book heartily recommended whole grains, olive oil, vegetables and fruits, nuts, and beans. Novel additions to his Healthy Eating Pyramid are alcohol in moderation (if appropriate)—depicted by a glass of red wine—daily exercise, and weight control.

Dr. Willett cited the low rates of heart disease and cancer among people eating a Mediterranean diet as solid proof of its safety. He also estimated that heart-disease rates in the United States could be reduced by at least 80 percent with moderate diet and lifestyle changes.

A study conducted by a group of researchers from the University of Barcelona set out to assess the effects of dietary changes on patients who were at high risk for heart disease. The participants in the study were between fifty-five and eighty years of age and had either type 2 diabetes or three or more risk factors for heart disease—such as smoking, hypertension, high cholesterol, and being overweight. After only three months on a Mediterranean diet, subjects experienced decreased blood pressure, improved lipid profiles, decreased insulin resistance, and reduced concentrations of inflammatory markers in their blood samples; all important predictors of chronic disease. This is especially impressive because three months is a relatively short period of time. And it encourages those of us with known risk factors who may be starting our quest for better health. Studies such as this have contributed to

Positive health requires a knowledge of man's primary constitution and of the powers of various foods. . . . But eating alone is not enough for health. There must also be exercise, of which the efforts must likewise be known. . . . If there is any deficiency in food or exercise, the body will fall sick. (Hippocrates, c. 460–377 B.C.E.)

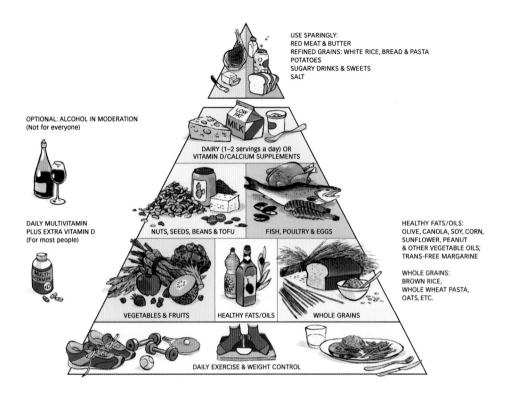

The Healthy Eating Pyramid.

Copyright 2008. For more information about the Healthy Eating Pyramid, please see The Nutrition Source, Department of Nutrition, Harvard School of Public Health, http://www.thenutritionsource.org and *Eat, Drink, and Be Healthy*, by Walter C. Willett, M.D., and Patrick J. Skerrett (2005), Free Press / Simon & Schuster Inc.

my belief that lifestyle changes not only keep us healthy but can change the course of disease (Estruch and others, "Effects of a Mediterranean-Style Diet," 1–11). A further assessment of the effects of the Mediterranean diet on Americans, through the National Institutes of Health–AARP Diet and Health Study, indicates that higher adherence to the Mediterranean diet is associated with lower death rates from all causes, including cancer and cardiovascular disease (Mitrou and others, "Mediterranean Diet Pattern").

Other studies have confirmed that closer adherence to the Mediterranean diet yields more extensive health benefits. As part of the European Prospective Investigation into Cancer, Dr. Dimitrios Trichopoulos of Harvard University studied twenty-six thousand Greek men and women and determined that those who most closely followed a Mediterranean diet were overall less likely to develop cancer (Benetou and others, "Conformity to Traditional Mediterranean Diet").

Dementia and Alzheimer's disease have us all concerned as our society ages and we begin to worry about our memories. Columbia University researchers recently discovered that people who followed a Mediterranean diet had a lower risk for developing mild cognitive impairment. Close adherence to the Mediterranean diet was associated with a 28 percent lower risk. In addition those who already had mild cognitive impairment and followed the Mediterranean diet most closely were 48 percent less likely to develop Alzheimer's disease. Though more research is necessary to confirm the role diet plays in reducing the risk of dementia, this would certainly be a wonderful benefit of eating foods we enjoy anyway (Scarmeas and others, "Mediterranean Diet").

The reduction of neural-tube birth defects such as spina bifida has been associated with a high consumption of folates before and during pregnancy. Folates are found in green leafy vegetables, fruits, beans, and peas, all of which are widely consumed in the traditional Greek diet. The lower rates of neural-tube defects in some Mediterranean countries suggest that the diet is beneficial for prevention (Christianson and others, *March of Dimes Global Report*).

Another prenatal benefit of the Mediterranean diet appears in a study by Greek researchers who compared pregnant women who adhered closely to a traditional Mediterranean diet with those who did not. The former group gave birth to children who by the age of six years, had developed asthma and allergies at much lower rates than the children born to the women who had not eaten the traditional diet (Chatzi and others, "Mediterranean Diet").

Yet another study followed schoolchildren on Crete over time and found that the children who consumed the traditional Greek diet had fewer allergy symptoms (rhinitis, dry cough, and wheezing). Eating grapes, apples, oranges, fresh tomatoes, and nuts was identified as protective against such symptoms (Chatzi and others, "Protective Effects").

With all the positive research findings pointing to the myriad health benefits of a traditional Greek diet, of late we hear alarming reports concerning nutrition in Greece. Fewer Mediterranean people are consuming the Mediterranean diet. In July 2008 ABC News was among the first to report that the United Nations Food and Agriculture Organization's senior economist had stated that Mediterranean people are currently consuming a diet that is "too fat, too salty, and too sweet."

It seems that, just as in the United States, more Mediterraneans are consuming more calories, expending fewer calories, and eating more meats, processed foods, and sugar than their ancestors did. Unfortunately the results are readily evident. More Mediterranean people are overweight and obese—with all the related health problems.

Even Greek children are getting fatter and experiencing high blood pressure, high cholesterol, and diabetes related to an increased consumption of convenience and fast foods. In a place where people were once fit and trim, enjoying active lives to very old age, the children are now experiencing such health problems that their life expectancy will be shorter than their parents' (Angelopoulos and others, "Relations between Obesity and Hypertension"; Rosenthal, "Fast Food Hits the Mediterranean"). Fifty years of research support the idea that the traditional Greek diet is an important source of health. And we now have evidence of the hazards associated with the abandonment of the traditional Mediterranean diet for the lure of fast food. One Greek gentleman interviewed for the *New York Times* was so upset about the changing eating habits of his family that he decided to buy a farm and grow his own traditional crops. Even today's Greeks need a Greek Revival!

THE TRADITIONAL GREEK DIET

So how do we define the "traditional Greek diet" or the "Mediterranean diet"? The following is a list of its basic elements developed by Antonia Trichopoulou of the University of Athens Medical School:

The Basic Characteristics of the Traditional Greek Diet

1. High consumption of olive oil
2. High consumption of legumes
3. High consumption of unrefined cereals (grains)
4. High consumption of fruits
5. High consumption of vegetables
6. Moderate consumption of dairy products, mostly as cheese and yogurt
7. Moderate to high consumption of fish
8. Low consumption of meat and meat products
9. Moderate consumption of wine

Dr. Trichopoulou's research stresses the *patterns* of eating these foods and *closely adhering* to the basic characteristics of the diet as being significant to the findings of positive health outcomes. Her studies also indicate that rather than single foods or nutrients, the *synergy* of the foods eaten in combination with one another, may be significant to achieving the many benefits of the traditional Greek diet (Trichopoulou and others, "Traditional Foods").

THE SOURCE OF FLAVOR AND HEALTH:
OLIVE OIL, NATURE'S GOLD

As the main source of fat in the Greek diet, olive oil has been recognized by various researchers as a contributing factor in the diet's protection against

Evidence points to the olive being cultivated on Crete as early as 2500 B.C. A remarkable feature at the palace of Knossos was the Room of the Olive Press, with open pipes that fed into storage vats. (Peggy Knickerbocker, Olive Oil from Tree to Table)

Ancient (3,000–2,000 B.C.E.) olive-oil jars at the Minoan Palace of Knossos, Crete. Photograph by Harris Pastides

[The olive] produces by the simplest of methods, the purest and most healthful oil available. Within the pulp of the red-ripe olive are small cellules containing wholesome, quite edible oil that can be extracted simply by pressing. Consequently, the vitamins that many other oils lose in chemical extraction and heat . . . purification are left unspoiled in cold-pressed, virgin olive oils, which are rich in Vitamins E and K and in beta carotenes. (Maggie Blyth Klein, The Feast of the Olive)

heart disease, atherosclerosis, diabetes, colon cancer, asthma, breast cancer, high blood pressure, osteoporosis, rheumatoid arthritis, dementia, and age-related blindness. Olive oil is a "good oil," arguably the best. In addition to the high concentration of oleic acid, it contains strong antioxidants, which also and lower cholesterol (Simopoulos and Robinson, *The Omega Diet*). Extra-virgin, cold-pressed olive oil has the highest content of nutrients because heat is not required for the extraction process. To keep olive oil at its peak nutritional quality there are a few things that are good to know.

Store the oil in a cool, dark place, not in sunlight. Olive oil is light sensitive, and there's some evidence that it loses nutritional value if it is exposed to light or is kept too long. Since I use a lot of olive oil, I buy it in large cans and decant it into a dark green glass bottle with a cork. I store it in a kitchen cabinet, out of direct sunlight.

Don't store olive oil in the refrigerator, as it will become solid. As it warms to room temperature it will liquefy, which may cause condensation to form inside the container. Any resulting drips of water could change the flavor of the oil or promote spoiling (Knickerbocker, *Olive Oil*, 29).

Olive oil adds a rich flavor to all foods, especially vegetables, salads, grain dishes, fish, and even meats. I think one of the reasons why Americans love Greek food is because the flavors of nearly all foods are enhanced by olive oil. Olive oil flows freely in Greek cuisine and so do the associated health benefits. While we don't want to overeat or consume more calories than we burn, we do need to be aware that a diet rich in olive oil and low in saturated fats has been shown to be healthier than a low-fat diet in a variety of ways, including for weight loss and diabetes control (Guttersen, "Weighing in on Obesity").

THE GREEK LIFESTYLE

There are two freeing and wonderful aspects of following a traditional Greek diet and lifestyle. The first is that the foods are fresh and delicious. The second is that the Greek lifestyle is not one of deprivation. Greeks do not *traditionally* eliminate foods from their diet. Because of the emphasis on plant-based foods, food is not weighed or measured. Because of the variety, foods are not eliminated or sworn off. Because mainly healthful fats are eaten, grams of fat are not calculated. Because whole grains are consumed, carbohydrates are not shunned. How freeing it is that, by following traditional food choices and patterns, eating does not have to be analyzed but can simply be *enjoyed*. This promotes a happy relationship with food where meals are anticipated with joy, not anxiety, and they're eaten with gusto. One can feel sated and virtuous eating roasted vegetables with olive oil and crusty whole-grain bread. Choosing flavorful, healthful food can engender a healthier attitude toward eating. Then there's the "not so secret" ingredient to the health benefits of the Greek lifestyle: *time.*

If you've had the pleasure of a Mediterranean vacation, the highlights of your memories no doubt are the wonderful meals, the sun, the slower pace of life, the music, the beaches, and the clear waters of a calm sea. If you enjoyed a Greek island, you most likely saw old men in the *kafeneon* sipping coffee, working worry beads through their rough knobby fingers, and talking nonstop. I'm quite sure you also witnessed the great-grandmothers, *yiayias,* dressed all in black, often with crosses around their necks and scarves covering their heads. These pillars of traditional Greek families still shop, cook, clean house, and sweep—and whitewash the sidewalks. Surprisingly they are often well into their nineties.

Healthy life is long for the followers of the traditional Greek peasant diet; meat is reserved for a special occasion; fish is common; and vegetables from the garden are overflowing. The noon meal is the big one, and its plates and bowls and platters hold stewed, braised, caramelized, long-cooked vegetables and beans swimming in olive oil. There is always a sip of wine in a small juice glass, and fresh fruit follows every meal. Kilos of fruit are brought to the table. Whether it's watermelon, figs, or oranges, fruit is cut open and consumed only if judged perfect by the host.

After lunch is a quiet time. Blinds are closed to shutter homes from the high sun. Ceiling fans turn. Lights are dimmed, and families rest. Even those

January sun in Athens.
Photograph by Harris
Pastides

working outside the home typically return home for lunch and rest. Late afternoon is wake-up time, the *second morning* of the day. Refreshed and unstressed, workers set back to work; students return to school; and stores reopen for late afternoon and evening shoppers.

A NEW GREEK REVIVAL?

Can we have a Greek Revival in the United States today? I think we can and we must. To join this revival, know the basic principles of the traditional Greek diet and let those principles guide your food choices. Trust the research. The news just keeps getting better. Cook. Employ the cooking methods described in this book. Remember that extra-virgin olive oil equals flavor. Adjust your food choices to maximize variety: grow your own vegetables or buy locally grown from small farms; seek out animal products from farms where the animals graze and are not subject to antibiotics or growth hormones. As for lifestyle, if our intention is to pattern our lives after the healthiest Greeks, we would exercise daily—get out and walk and take in some sunshine. We would take time for the people important to us. Talk with family and friends, share, discuss, challenge, and support each other. And rest, even during the most hectic of days. Most of us can't go home and nap, but we can close the door; close the world out for fifteen minutes. Take a few deep breaths . . . a *hypnogogic* nap. Or take a short walk, a physical break, in the afternoon. It is possible to be refreshed and renewed during busy days, if we choose the right tools.

The Church of 100 Bells with oranges in Paros. Photograph by Harris Pastides

PROLOGUE

Breakfast on Sifnos

◻

Creamy Yogurt with Fruit and Nuts—Sifnos Breakfast

ON A FAMILY TRIP TO GREECE, a certain breakfast became lusciously important to me. We were traveling with another family, dear friends. Together we were four adults and five children ages eight to thirteen.

We'd spent several sticky days sightseeing in Athens, bartering in Plaka for souvenirs, being jostled on the subway, and standing in a long line to taste Thanassi's *souvlaki*. Seeing the Acropolis was a thrill, especially for the boys, since in those days you could crawl all over the ruins. The dads talked architecture, scale, angles, and missing caryatids. The girls took pictures of the boys (not our boys)! The moms applied sunscreen and chided the boys, who climbed perilously high on piles of marble. After a few such days, the ferry to Paros was a welcome captivity, a slow ride but cool and breezy. There was a bag of plums and another of cheese pies to hold us, but once the concession bar was discovered, we were coerced into chips and Oranginas. On Paros we spent long days on the beach, coming up at one for a leisurely *taverna* meal. One child ate nothing but french fries. The rest of us ate everything they served everyday starting with plates of tomato-and-cucumber salad with plenty of bread to soak up the well of olive oil in the bottom of the dish. *Kadema* was the afternoon beach game—two paddles and a small ball—son versus son, son versus father, and, most competitive, father versus father. Every day the record of volleys without a miss got higher. Sometimes a second look at a bathing beauty was all it took to ruin a high score. Sunbathing was manageable, punctuated by cooling dips in aqua water. Novels were devoured, and the girls read fashion magazines. When we'd had enough, we went off to our respective family rooms, showered in a steadily decreasing stream of water, and then napped well into the evening, in training for dinners that started at 10:00 P.M.

After Paros we went on to Sifnos by hydrofoil. Unlike the lazy ferry, this was a speedy trip—flying just on the surface of the water in a compact low-ceiling speedboat, belted in airplane-style seats. One of the children threw up. The uniformed stewardesses with blue-and-yellow scarves passed out mints. We hit the fogged-in island at about midnight, urging sleeping children to drag their bags up a winding road to find Michalis's pensione—in the pitch dark. We fell into the beds. In the morning a sparkling Sifnos revealed itself, a less touristy, diminutive, working island in the Cycladic group with narrow roads, steep cliffs, and private beaches in protective coves. Its scruffy, hilly landscape was dotted with round-domed chapels crowned with white crosses against a blue cloudless sky.

We needed transportation to explore this new terrain, so the dads went off to rent cars. They returned with "the donkeys," two little tin cans of cars that we drove in tandem by day, winding our way up steep hills and down again, and "tied up" at night to "graze" in a dirt parking lot.

My children had their dad. The other dad had his friend. Just one thing was missing: I'd "lost" my husband. By the time we reached Sifnos, this problem had been diagnosed. And it was clear that nobody else liked getting up early, so early was our chance. We rose at 6:00 A.M., walked down a dirt path to the sea, and swam. It became a ritual. We swam side by side until one of us issued a challenge by taking off; then we raced. The water felt warmer than the air, so we treaded water up to our shoulders until we saw the *taverna* owner making coffee. Then we bolted to the rocky beach, wrapped up in Michalis's towels, and became the first *taverna* customers. We ordered filtered coffee and thick, plain yogurt—sinfully creamy and loaded with grapes and walnuts. Thyme honey was poured on top and cascaded down the sides of the bowls. We sat there and ate until our bowls gleamed clean white and our coffee cups were filled twice and emptied. The following recipe is that simple and satisfying breakfast we enjoyed for five consecutive mornings, feeling fortunate to be on Sifnos together.

Creamy Yogurt with Fruit and Nuts—Sifnos Breakfast

Straining plain yogurt creates a thick and creamy yogurt with the flavor of traditional Greek yogurt but with much less fat. The resulting liquid contains protein and can be used in other recipes. One idea is to add it to soups. For variety you can substitute any fresh fruit for the grapes—peaches, strawberries, and bananas are all delicious. Also try different chopped nuts—your imagination is the only limit to this easy, healthful, and satisfying breakfast.

1 quart plain yogurt
   (nonfat tastes fine)
1 cup green seedless grapes
1 cup shelled walnuts
Honey (drizzle to taste)

STRAIN THE YOGURT through a fine mesh sieve or cheesecloth for 20–30 minutes in the refrigerator. The resulting liquid can be discarded or reserved for another use.

Cut the grapes in half, or if they are very large, cut them in quarters and set them aside. Roughly chop the shelled walnuts and set them aside.

When the yogurt is strained, spoon about ¾ cup of yogurt into each bowl. Top the yogurt with halved grapes and sprinkle with chopped walnuts. Finally drizzle honey over the top.

Serves 4–6

Grape Leaves Stuffed with Cracked Wheat and Pine Nuts—*Dolmades*, p. 30

1. APPETIZERS—*MEZEDAKIA*

Greek Caviar—*Taramosalata*

Yogurt, Garlic, and Cucumber Dip—*Tzatziki*

Roasted Red-Pepper and Feta Dip

Cheese and Mint Pie—*Tiropita*

Sautéed Dates with Almonds

Spinach and Dill Pie—*Spanakopita*

Broccoli and Blue-Cheese *Pita*

Onion and Beet-Green *Pita*

Crispy Cypriot Sheep Cheese with Lemon—*Haloumi*

Creamy Garlic Sauce—*Skordalia*

Warm Feta, Tomato, and Oregano—*Saganaki*

Grape Leaves Stuffed with Cracked Wheat and Pine Nuts—*Dolmades*

Coriander and Garlic Olives—*Elies Tsakistes*

Chickpeas with Onion and White Wine—*Revithia*

IN THE TRADITIONAL GREEK WAY OF EATING, one can have a series of appetizers, *mezes,* either preceding the main course or as the entire dinner. This is a lovely way to eat to enjoy a variety of flavors and food groups.

One of the best things about *taverna*-style dining in Greece is the speed with which the food is served. No sooner do you order than the waiter appears with at least six small plates balanced on an outstretched arm and flings the plates like Frisbees onto the table while naming the dishes: *"yogourrt and cucoomber deep, feesh eggs salata, eggplants salata, oaktopouss, squeeds, leetle feeshies."* He may even proclaim *"brrrread and wat-ter!"*

A POTENT MEDICINE: GARLIC

You will find that garlic is used in recipes throughout this book. For many people garlic makes everything taste better. In her classic *Book of Mediterranean Food,* first published in Britain in 1950, Elizabeth David quotes chef, restaurateur, author, and BBC cooking-show host (circa 1937) Marcel Boulestin: "It is not really an exaggeration to say that peace and happiness begin, geographically, where garlic is used in cooking" (David, *A Book of Mediterranean Food,* xv). If that's not enough of a reason to use this pungent member of the lily family, there are many health benefits to convince you: "Through history garlic has been known to be a potent medicine providing protection from many types of disease. Ancient Greek and Roman soldiers were given a ration of garlic each day. It has antiseptic properties, which are purported to prevent infection and the formation of harmful bacteria in the stomach and intestines" (Garland, *The Complete Book of Herbs and Spices,* 27–28).

Garlic has traditionally been associated with the peasant diet, which we now see as a good thing. But in class-conscious societies garlic was often avoided because of that association. Today consumption of garlic is encouraged for thinning the blood, reducing blood pressure, lowering cholesterol, improving immunity, fighting microbes, reducing chronic inflammation, and possibly protecting against cancer (Hyman and Liponis, *Ultraprevention*).

HOW'S MY *SKORDALIA*?

Probably one of my funnier cooking stories relates to those previously mentioned cooking classes in Athens. We had worked that day on dips: *tzatziki,* a delicious combination of thick yogurt, garlic, and cucumber; *taramosalata,* a dip created from red fish roe, bread, onion, and lemon; and *skordalia,* a garlic dip made with either bread or mashed potatoes and walnuts. Garlic is the predominant taste of *skordalia,* which calls for many cloves of fresh garlic.

A marble-store owner's mosaic creation, Paros. Photograph by Harris Pastides

As was the custom at the end of class, each student received some of the food to take home. At home I tucked the *skordalia* into the fridge. That evening we had plans to go out to dinner with our friend Giorgos. Giorgos arrived before the babysitter. I was bathing the children, so Harris offered him a drink. Then it dawned on me to show off my Greek cooking with an authentic Greek friend, so I called out,

"Why don't you let Giorgos try my *skordalia?* It's in the fridge." Then I added, "Giorgo, let me know what you think."

I waited, but no words of praise came from the kitchen. They had clearly tasted it, but it was just as clear from the suspended conversation that they were searching for another topic. I couldn't stand it:

"So Giorgo, what did you think of the *skordalia?*"

"Well," came the sheepish reply, "it's a little bland."

"BLAND, how can it be bland? It has five cloves of garlic!" With that I raced into the kitchen to defend my dip, and discovered that my dear husband had served our friend leftover pancake batter from the children's breakfast!

I guarantee that, with the following recipes, your garlicky dips, savory *pitas,* and tangy *dolmades* will never be described as "bland." But just to be sure, I recommend serving them yourself.

Greek Caviar—*Taramosalata*

Unusual in color, this recipe is a standout on a buffet!

PROCESS THE FISH ROE (*tarama*) and the lemon juice in a food processor fitted with a steel blade. Squeeze the water from the bread and discard the water. Add half the bread to the food processor, process, then pour in half the olive oil and process again. Add the remaining bread, process, then add the last of the olive oil and process all until smooth. The *taramosalata* will be pink to salmon colored.

This is a recipe that should be adjusted to one's taste. You may like to add more lemon juice or top the dip with a little grated onion.

You can serve this recipe as you would any dip, with raw vegetables or toasted pita bread. I have served it in cherry tomatoes, cutting off the tops and hollowing them out. This makes a pretty presentation when each is topped with a tiny sprig of chopped dill.

6 ounces red fish roe
(usually carp or codfish roe)

Juice of one lemon

6 slices stale whole-grain
bread without crusts,
soaked in water

$\frac{1}{2}$ cup olive oil

Yogurt, Garlic, and Cucumber Dip—*Tzatziki*

A favorite and versatile Greek dip, *tzatziki* can be enjoyed simply with bread or crudités but is also the perfect accompaniment to grilled meats. Many Americans are familiar with a version of *tzatziki* that is served with *gyros* (spiced ground lamb, grilled, topped with raw onion and *tzatziki*, and served in pita bread). The foundation for *tzatziki* is a thick, creamy yogurt in which lots of spicy minced garlic is balanced by the clean taste of grated cucumber and sea salt. This basic *tzatziki*, found in every *taverna* in Greece, is typically customized by the chef's choice of a chopped herb, which adds a fresh brightness to its intense flavor.

In Greece a thick homemade yogurt is used for *tzatziki*. Unfortunately some restaurateurs in the United States have used sour cream. It has a comparable texture, but it lacks the tart tanginess of yogurt and adds additional saturated fat to the *tzatziki*.

My solution is to strain my favorite plain yogurt to remove the whey, which is the liquid. Straining the yogurt renders a thick creamy, much more authentic tasting base for *tzatziki*.

---

1 quart plain yogurt (nonfat or low fat is fine)

1 large cucumber

3 cloves garlic, minced

¼ cup fresh dill, chopped

Sea salt

TRANSFER THE YOGURT to a fine mesh strainer or cheesecloth and strain in the refrigerator for 20 minutes to 3 hours.

Peel the cucumber and cut it in half lengthwise. Scoop out the seeds with a teaspoon. Grate the cucumber with a box grater using the larger holes. When it is grated, squeeze as much water out of the cucumber as you can. Place the grated cucumber in a fine mesh strainer over a bowl. Lightly salt the grated cucumber and set it in the refrigerator to drain until the yogurt is ready.

When the yogurt has drained, discard the liquid. Combine the thick yogurt, cucumber, minced garlic, and dill. Stir to combine. Add sea salt to taste.

When serving the *tzatziki,* you may drizzle it with olive oil if you wish. Serve it with crusty bread, pita bread, or crudités—or with grilled lamb, chicken, or pork.

Roasted Red-Pepper and Feta Dip

This recipe combines the sweetness of the peppers with the tanginess of the feta cheese, and you can add heat with a sprinkle of red-pepper flakes if you wish.

2 roasted red bell peppers

3 tablespoons olive oil

2 cloves garlic, minced

$\frac{1}{4}$ teaspoon red-pepper flakes (optional)

8 ounces sheep's milk feta cheese, crumbled

PUREE THE ROASTED RED PEPPERS in a food processor.

Heat the olive oil over medium-high heat and lightly brown the minced garlic. As the garlic is just browning, add the red-pepper flakes and toss just a few times to combine the flavors. Remove the pan from the heat.

Add the oil-and-garlic mixture and the crumbled feta to the pureed peppers in the food processor and process until well blended.

Transfer the Roasted Red-Pepper and Feta Dip to a serving bowl and refrigerate before serving. Serve with whole-grain pita bread or crudités.

Roasted Red-Pepper and Feta Dip also makes a luscious sandwich when topped with sliced avocados.

ROASTING PEPPERS

Roasted red peppers are a wonderful addition to sandwiches and salads. And peppers are easy to roast under your broiler.

All you have to do is preheat your broiler and prick the whole peppers five or six times in various places with a fork. Place them on a broiler pan as close to the heat as possible. When the top sides have blackened, turn the peppers. Continue broiling and turning them until they have blackened all around. Remove the roasted peppers from the broiler, place them in a paper bag, roll down the top of the bag, and let them cool inside the bag. When they are cool enough to handle, remove the peppers from the bag and peel off the blackened outer skin, which will pull off easily.

Cut off the stems, remove the seeds, and slice; they are ready to use in any recipe, or to eat by themselves.

Cheese and Mint Pie—*Tiropita*

There are many different recipes for cheese pies. My mother-in-law wasn't very fond of feta cheese, so she made her *tiropita* with ricotta and cream cheese. Though less traditional, her *tiropita* was always enjoyed by family and friends. In the following recipe, the fresh mint is the "secret ingredient" that makes this cheese pie a standout. The mint complements the tanginess of the feta and brightens the flavor. I prefer using all butter to make these pies because it renders the filo dough lighter and flakier. But if you need to restrict your intake of saturated fat, you may use olive or canola oil or blend one of these oils with some melted butter.

Filo is purchased frozen from the market. Thaw it in the refrigerator for at least 24 hours before use. I have used it successfully for up to 4 weeks after thawing in refrigerator. The consistency of filo can vary depending on how long it's been in the grocer's freezer. Sometimes it can be a bit too dry to make individual pies. If I find this to be the case, instead of making individual pies, I make a large cheese pie in a 9 x 11-inch baking pan, which is much more forgiving!

To make one large *tiropita,* follow the directions for assembling and baking the dinner-entrée version of *spanakopita* on page 21.

PREHEAT THE OVEN to 400 degrees.

Combine crumbled feta cheese, ricotta cheese, eggs, chopped mint leaves, and black pepper in a bowl. Stir to mix well and set aside.

Melt butter over low heat and get your pastry brush ready. I've discovered that small paint brushes (1–2 inches) work well.

Open the filo package and remove one roll. Remove the plastic packaging around the roll. The roll of filo will be wrapped in waxed paper; leave it on there for now. With a sharp serrated knife, cut through the roll to make three equal parts. Place a sheet of waxed paper on your work surface. Roll one section of filo out onto the waxed paper with the width near you and the length spread out directly in front of you. Place the other two sections of filo, which are not currently in use, in the refrigerator wrapped in a kitchen towel. Return the second roll of filo to the refrigerator as well. You should take out only one section at a time so the filo will remain chilled and not become soggy.

Brush melted butter on the top sheet of filo. Place 1 tablespoon of filling at the end closest to you. From the left corner of the filo dough lift up 2 sheets together and fold them from that corner across the dough to meet the right edge of the dough. Next fold the piece straight up and then across to the left. Continue folding up and then across to make the triangle. Do you remember how to fold a flag? It's the same method. It will be easier if you adjust the filling by pressing slightly on the filo so the cheese fills in the triangle. When you've folded the first one about half way, brush it again with butter. Continue folding until you have a perfect triangle and brush the front and back with butter. If at first these are a bit messy, don't be discouraged. Practice does make perfect, and you will get there!

At this point place the finished *tiropita* on an ungreased baking sheet leaving a little space between each one. When the sheet is full, you can

1 pound feta cheese, crumbled (sheep's milk feta cheese is preferable)

2 cups ricotta cheese (part skim)

2 eggs (for an extra nutritional boost, use omega-3 eggs)

½ cup fresh mint leaves without stems, washed and chopped small

½ teaspoon black pepper

¾ cup butter, melted

1 pound prepared, frozen filo dough thawed in refrigerator for 24 hours before using

Omega-3 eggs are produced by chickens that are fed a diet containing grains, soy protein, and flax and enriched with vitamin E. The resulting eggs contain extra omega-3 fatty acids. There are several brands of these eggs available today. For more information on omega-3 fatty acids see chapter 2: Vegetable Dishes and chapter 4: Seafood.

bake them. They will be done when they are a deep golden brown and smell really good (approximately 20 minutes).

Makes about 50 triangles

FREEZING *TIROPITA*

If you wish to freeze some *tiropita*, layer them in a plastic freezer container with a sheet of waxed paper between layers so they don't lose their shape. I've kept them in my freezer for 2–3 weeks. They freeze and bake well.

To bake frozen *tiropita*, remove them from the freezer and place them on an ungreased baking sheet while still frozen. Do not thaw them first. Bake in a preheated 400-degree oven about 20 minutes. They may take a minute or two longer than freshly made *tiropita*, but not much.

Sautéed Dates with Almonds

This recipe makes a delicious snack for your guests for cocktail hour. It is a Mediterranean recipe, though I was introduced to it, not in Greece, but in Provence at the cooking school of Patricia Wells.

EXAMINE A DATE to locate the hole from which the pit was extracted. Insert a whole roasted almond into the hole. Repeat until you have made the desired number of stuffed dates. Heat a drizzle of olive oil in a sauté pan over medium heat. Sauté the stuffed dates for a few minutes, then turn them and sauté for a few more minutes. The dates will soften and slightly deepen in color.

Remove the stuffed dates from the pan to a serving dish and sprinkle with sea salt. Serve immediately.

Dried pitted dates
Roasted whole almonds
Olive oil
Sea salt

These Sautéed Dates with Almonds have that wonderful sweet and salty combination taste and are sure to stimulate your guests' appetites.

Spinach and Dill Pie— *Spanakopita*

When we returned from our sabbatical in Greece back in the late 1980s, we threw a Greek-themed dinner party, complete with many of the dishes I had learned to make in Greece. In those days we had a lot of neighborhood "potluck" suppers, and whenever someone hosted one, we'd all bring something. After our Greek party, *spanakopita* became the most popular food that I was asked to bring to parties. It remains a favorite today.

Spanakopita has become a well-known item with caterers as a passed hors d'oeuvre, usually shaped in small triangles. Commercially prepared versions can be found in freezer cases of many markets. You can also make *spanakopita* as a dinner entrée in a 9 x 11-inch pan, which has a faster preparation time.

---

6 cups (10 ounces) fresh baby-spinach leaves

8 ounces sheep's milk feta cheese, crumbled

1/3 cup finely chopped fresh dill

1 egg, slightly beaten

Sea salt and pepper to taste

1/2 cup butter, melted

1/2 pound prepared, frozen filo dough thawed in refrigerator for 24 before using

PREHEAT THE OVEN to 400 degrees.

Roughly chop the baby spinach leaves just to release their flavor. Place the chopped baby spinach in a large mixing bowl. Add the crumbled feta cheese, chopped dill, and slightly beaten egg. Add a bit of sea salt and pepper if desired. In the traditional Greek way—with clean hands—thoroughly combine the spinach, feta, dill, egg, sea salt, and pepper. Set aside.

To make *spanakopita* triangles, follow directions for folding, buttering, and baking Cheese and Mint Pie—*Tiropita* on page 17.

Makes about 30 triangles

SPANAKOPITA ENTRÉE

To make the dinner-entrée-size *spanakopita,* prepare the spinach filling as directed in the recipe.

Butter the bottom of a 9 x 11-inch baking pan, then layer whole sheets of filo dough one at a time, brushing each sheet with melted butter. When you have layered about half the roll of filo, spread the *spanako-pita* filling evenly on the filo.

Resume layering and buttering the second half of the sheets of filo, until you have used that entire roll.

Using your brush, tuck all the overhanging edges of filo down into the sides of the pan. This will create a nice brown edge all around the *spanakopita* when it is baked.

Before baking, cut the *spanakopita* into the desired number of pieces, being careful to cut all the way through to the pan. This will allow the moisture from the spinach to escape during baking and will make the filo crispy.

Bake the *spanakopita* in a 400-degree oven for approximately 30 minutes, or until it is well browned.

A large slice of spanakopita makes a fine dinner entrée when served with a salad or other vegetable dishes of your choice.

Broccoli and Blue-Cheese *Pita*

A variation on a theme, Broccoli and Blue-Cheese *Pita* is a new recipe based on traditional *spanakopita*. This is an example of how you can combine your favorite flavors and create your own recipe for a unique *pita*.

---

1 head broccoli (thick stems discarded), chopped small

2 medium onions, chopped small

2 tablespoons olive oil

4 ounces blue cheese, crumbled

4 ounces fresh mozzarella cheese, grated in food processor

1 egg, slightly beaten

¼ cup fresh parsley, finely chopped

½ pound prepared, frozen filo dough, thawed in refrigerator for 24 hours before using

6 tablespoons butter, melted

Sea salt and pepper

PREHEAT THE OVEN to 375 degrees.

Boil broccoli until tender, drain and set aside.

In a medium saucepan, heat 2 tablespoons of olive oil and sauté the chopped onions until soft and golden. Set aside to cool.

In a mixing bowl, combine crumbled blue cheese, grated mozzarella cheese, the beaten egg, and chopped parsley. Add sea salt and pepper to taste.

When the broccoli and onions have cooled, place them in the bowl of a food processor. Process into a thick paste.

Blend this paste into the bowl with the cheese mixture.

In a 9 x 11-inch pan, layer 6–8 sheets of filo dough, lightly buttering each, then spread half the cheese and broccoli filling over the filo. Top with 4 additional sheets of filo, buttering each, then spread this filo with the remainder of the filling. Finally top with 6–8 sheets of filo, buttering each.

Cut the Broccoli and Blue-Cheese *Pita* into the desired number of pieces, making sure to cut through to the pan so steam can escape. Bake for 45 minutes until golden brown.

Serves 6–8

This pita *is lovely when served with a green salad for lunch or a light dinner, or it may be served as an appetizer or side dish. It can be served directly from the oven or at room temperature.*

Onion and Beet-Green *Pita*

There truly is no limit to the fillings you can create for your *pitas*. In this case I hated to throw away the beet greens after making roasted beets, so I didn't. Instead I created a *pita* that incorporates the greens and stems with slowly sautéed onions, which become sweet, and just a touch of blue cheese for pizzazz.

¼ cup olive oil

3 medium onions, thinly sliced

1 cup beet-green stems, washed and chopped small

5 cups julienned beet greens (from 2 small bunches of fresh beets), washed, dried, and generously sprinkled with sea salt and pepper

3–4 ounces blue cheese, crumbled

½ pound frozen, prepared filo dough, thawed in refrigerator for 24 hours before using

6 tablespoons butter

PREHEAT THE OVEN to 400 degrees.

Heat ¼ cup olive oil in a large sauté pan over medium heat. Add the sliced onions and the chopped beet-green stems. Lower the heat and sauté the onions and stems over low heat until the onions are caramelized, about 35 minutes. When the onions are soft and brown and the stems are soft, add the julienned greens and cook over medium heat for another 8–10 minutes, tossing to combine, until the greens wilt. Water will be drawn from the greens; after they wilt, lower the heat and continue cooking for another 10 minutes, until most of the water evaporates.

Remove the pan from the heat and set aside.

Butter the bottom of a 9 x 11-inch pan. Layer filo, brushing each sheet lightly with melted butter until half the filo fills the bottom of the pan. Spoon the onion and beet-green filling on top of filo, then dot with 3–4 ounces of blue cheese. Resume layering and buttering the filo until finished, then tuck all edges in with the buttered brush.

Cut the Onion and Beet-Green *Pita* into small pieces all the way through to the pan. Bake in a 400-degree oven for 25–30 minutes until the top is well browned.

Serve warm as an appetizer or side dish.

Serves 10–12

Crispy Cypriot Sheep Cheese with Lemon—*Haloumi*

Haloumi is as popular in Cyprus as *feta* is in Greece. Greek Cypriots love their *haloumi*. They order it as an appetizer with every *taverna* dinner and serve it uncooked with watermelon for a light lunch or late-night summer supper. *Haloumi* is available in many American cheese shops and supermarkets that offer imported cheeses.

1 block imported *haloumi* (about 11 ounces)

1 teaspoon olive oil
1 lemon, cut into wedges
2 whole-wheat pita breads, cut into wedges

Haloumi *is a semihard cheese, which can be fried or grilled without melting into a puddle. It is made with mint, which gives it a wonderfully fresh taste.*

SLICE THE BLOCK of *haloumi* lengthwise into ⅓-inch slices. Heat 1 teaspoon of olive oil over medium-high heat in a frying pan. Place the slices of *haloumi* in a moderately hot pan and fry for a few minutes. If the olive oil begins to smoke, lower the heat a bit. Don't turn the slices until the cheese feels firm. Carefully check by lifting one piece with tongs to see if the pan side has browned. When the pan side is brown, carefully turn each piece and fry the other side. The *haloumi* will become a beautiful golden brown on both sides and will remain firm.

Place a piece of *haloumi* on each wedge of pita bread and top with a squeeze of fresh lemon juice. Serve immediately.

Haloumi is delicious garnished with fresh basil leaves and served with quartered fresh figs.

Fried *haloumi* is also wonderful served atop any salad—see Arugula and *Haloumi* Salad (page 52)—or on a sandwich—see *Haloumi* and Basil Sandwich (page 168).

Serves 4–8 as an appetizer

Creamy Garlic Sauce— *Skordalia*

Skordalia is a garlicky dip for raw vegetables, and it is also commonly served as a sauce with any type of fish.

TRIM ALL HARD CRUST from the bread and set aside. Soak the bread in a bowl of warm water briefly. Then squeeze the water from the bread, discard the water, and set the bread aside.

In a food processor, grind the walnuts, then process well after adding each of the following ingredients: garlic, damp bread, lemon juice, and olive oil. Continue processing until all ingredients are combined into a smooth sauce. Add sea salt and pepper to taste. If your bread is particularly dense, you may need to add more olive oil.

For color, garnish with fresh basil.

3 cups stale bread (any leftover bread that is not sweet;
  dense and crusty bread
  works well)
$3/4$ cup walnut pieces
5 cloves garlic
2 tablespoons fresh lemon
  juice
$1/2$ cup olive oil
Sea salt and pepper
Fresh basil for garnish

Bread crusts may be ground into bread crumbs for future use.

Warm Feta, Tomato, and Oregano—*Saganaki*

I tasted my first *saganaki* at a Greek restaurant in New Haven, Connecticut. Not only did it serve authentic Greek fare, but on Friday and Saturday nights at ten, this restaurant offered Greek folk dancing right in the dining room. Tables and chairs were moved; bouzouki, mandolin, and accordion music filled the room; and the owner herself led the patrons in circle dances such as the *sirtaki*, made famous in the film *Zorba the Greek*. It started off slowly, then gradually sped up until arms were clutching others tightly, just to hold on as the room flew in circles. Great fun, but not recommended on a full stomach!

One evening, shortly after Harris and I met, he took me to this restaurant for my first Greek feast, an initiation that proved to be full of warmth, color, flavor, and lots of lively people. He ordered several *mezedakia*, little starter plates; one had the jarring title "flaming *saganaki!*" The waiter brought a square of hard cheese on a small metal tray, squirted some liquid over it (which to this day Harris teases was lighter fluid), and lit it with a match! What a show! I was impressed. But I remember the flames more than the flavor, and that says something.

For a change, Warm Feta, Tomato, and Oregano—Saganaki also makes a delicious pasta or pizza sauce.

Imagine my surprise years later in Cyprus when I tasted a delicious baked feta smothered in tomatoes and oregano—not flambéed but warm so that all the flavors merged in the mouth—and was told it was "*saganaki.*" The following recipe provides a simple method to achieve that savory baked *saganaki* taste.

HEAT THE 2 TABLESPOONS OF OLIVE OIL over medium-high heat. Add chopped tomatoes and oregano and cook for several minutes, stirring occasionally until the tomatoes soften and their juice is released. Lower the heat to medium and cook until most of the juice has evaporated. This is important because, once the tomato juice has evaporated, the concentrated tomatoes that remain are full of savory flavor. Break the feta cheese into several small chunks and add it to pan. Cook just a few minutes more until the feta is well blended with the tomatoes and is beginning to melt.

Transfer the *feta saganaki* to a serving bowl and serve with crusty bread as an appetizer.

Serves 6–8

2 tablespoons olive oil

4 cups ripe tomatoes, chopped small

2 teaspoons dried oregano

8 ounces sheep's milk feta cheese

If local tomatoes are not in season, chopped or crushed canned tomatoes work well in this recipe when strained of excess juice.

Grape Leaves Stuffed with Cracked Wheat and Pine Nuts—*Dolmades*

Most *dolmades* are stuffed with ground meat and white rice or white rice and herbs. The following healthy version uses bulgur (cracked wheat), which is a whole grain without the saturated fat of ground meat. The cumin and pine nuts provide flavor, and the pine nuts add protein too. This dish is a great source of dietary fiber. But the best test of these *dolmades* is whether you can stuff the grape leaves before you've eaten all the filling!

HEARTLAND BULGUR

I like to use Heartland Bulgur. If you use it, you will need only 1 cup of boiling water. Pour the water over the bulgur and other ingredients you've added to it, stir, and cover. Remove the pan from the heat and let the bulgur rest this way for 30 minutes. The bulgur is ready when all the liquid is absorbed. This is easy, and the result is a fluffy bulgur that is never gummy.

REMOVE THE GRAPE LEAVES from their jar, strain off the liquid, and trim away remaining stems. Set aside.

Heat the olive oil in a large sauté pan over medium-high heat. Add the chopped onion and cook it until it is soft and transparent. Add the minced garlic, and stir in the pine nuts, cumin, and sea salt and pepper to taste. Lower the heat to medium and cook the mixture until the garlic is light brown. Next stir in the bulgur, boiling water, raisins, and half the lemon juice. Lower the heat and simmer uncovered, stirring occasionally, until almost all the liquid has evaporated. The bulgur should be tender. (If it is still hard, add another ½ cup boiling water and continue cooking until the bulgur is tender.) When the bulgur is fully cooked, remove the pan from the heat and stir in the chopped cilantro leaves to combine.

Prepare a medium-size saucepan by lining it with grape leaves to cover the bottom.

Set a pile of grape leaves out flat in front of you with the stem end closest to you and the veins facing up. Place a heaping tablespoon of filling at the stem end of the leaf, then fold each side in toward the center of the leaf. When both sides are folded in, roll the leaf away from you as tightly as possible until it makes a small, approximately 3-inch log. Place the stuffed grape leaf into the pan lined with grape leaves.

Continue rolling until you have no filling left and the pan is full of stuffed grape leaves. Pour enough water over the grape leaves to cover them, and place a heavy plate on top to keep the grape leaves from unrolling. Cover the pan and bring to a boil, then lower the heat and simmer for about 30 minutes.

Remove the pan from the heat and let it cool. When they are cool enough to handle, take the stuffed grape leaves from the pot and arrange them on a platter. Sprinkle with the remaining lemon juice and garnish with thin lemon slices. You may serve the *dolmades* at room temperature or chilled.

Makes about 25–30 *dolmades*

1 bottle cured grape leaves
2 tablespoons olive oil
1 medium onion, finely chopped
1 clove garlic, minced
¼ cup pine nuts
1 teaspoon cumin
Sea salt and pepper (optional)
1 cup bulgur
2 cups boiling water
2 tablespoons raisins
Juice of 1 lemon
¼ cup cilantro leaves, chopped
Thinly sliced lemon for garnish

Coriander and Garlic Olives—
Elies Tsakistes

I loved my mother-in-law's name, *Anastasia,* which means "the resurrection." I also loved that she referred to me through her thick accent as her "daughter-in-love," really believing that was the term.

Anastasia prepared some unbelievable olives. She bought them unripened—as hard as little stones—and cracked them with a hammer to create uneven openings in the fruit. She soaked them in salted water for at least a month, changing the water periodically, until they were soft enough to eat but still a bit firm. She started with a large jar of salted water. She told me the way to know how much salt to use is to place a whole raw egg, shell and all, in the bottom of the jar, fill the jar with water, then pour salt in until the egg floats to the top. Then you know you have the right amount of salt. When the egg floats, you remove it and put the olives in the jar.

After about a month, when they had softened to just the right texture, she set them in a savory marinade of crushed garlic, cracked coriander seeds, lemon juice, and olive oil. The following recipe closely approximates Anastasia's olives, although the texture is softer because it begins with olives that have already been commercially cured.

One brand of olives I've used is Greek Gourmet, which comes in a 6½-ounce glass jar.

Good, fruity olive oil is extra virgin and green in color with a lovely olive fragrance.

Greeks leave their olives on the counter, because the olive oil will solidify in the refrigerator. They don't generally last long enough to spoil.

STRAIN THE LIQUID from the olives and discard it, but save the jar. Place the olives in a bowl. Make a marinade by combining the olive oil, lemon juice, lemon wedges, crushed coriander seeds, and roughly chopped garlic. Stir to combine.

Return the olives and marinade to the jar. If the marinade doesn't fill the jar, add enough additional olive oil to fill the jar to the top. Put the lid on and turn it to secure tightly. Shake the jar to combine the liquids, which will separate.

Prepare *Elies Tsakistes* the day before you wish to serve them so the olives will have time to absorb the flavors of their new marinade.

1 jar (approximately 6½ ounces) green olives cured in salt and water
⅓ cup good fruity olive oil
Juice of ½ lemon
3–4 small lemon wedges with peel
1 tablespoon coriander seeds, coarsely crushed with mortar and pestle
3 cloves garlic, peeled, crushed, and rough chopped

Chickpeas with Onion and White Wine—*Revithia*

In Greece chickpeas, or *revithia,* are purchased dry like other beans. They are soaked and then cooked several hours in the oven at low heat so they become tender but not mushy. This recipe cuts the cooking time by using canned chickpeas. Since beans require a long cooking time to soften, there is not much nutritional difference between canned and dried beans. But read the can label to avoid additives such as large quantities of sodium.

With the fresh parsley, lemon juice, and hot pepper, *revithia* is a delicious and satisfying appetizer that has the added benefit of being nutritious and heart healthy. You can also add a cup of your favorite whole grain (brown rice, bulgur, or barley) to this recipe to create a vegetarian main dish that provides a healthy source of protein and a good dose of fiber.

STRAIN THE CANNED CHICKPEAS, reserve the liquid, and set aside.

Sauté the chopped onion in olive oil over medium-high heat until the onion is soft and translucent.

Add dried oregano, red-pepper flakes, white wine, and ½ cup of the liquid from the canned chickpeas. Stir together.

Next add the chickpeas and gently toss to combine. Lower the heat to simmer and let them cook for several minutes until most, but not all, of the liquid evaporates.

Spoon the *revithia* into a serving dish, squeeze lemon juice over the chickpeas, and top with parsley and lemon zest.

Revithia is eaten as an appetizer and does not need to be served hot.

Serves 8–10

2 15-ounce cans of chickpeas

3 tablespoons olive oil

1 large sweet onion, chopped small

2 teaspoons dried oregano

¼–½ teaspoon red-pepper flakes (to taste)

¼ cup dry white wine

½ cup liquid from canned chickpeas

Juice of ½ lemon

Grated lemon zest for garnish

⅓ cup fresh parsley, finely chopped, for garnish

Summer Vegetable Bake—
Briam, p. 60

2. VEGETABLE DISHES

■

Greek Salad—*Salata Horiatiki*
Cypriot Village Salad—*Salata Horiatiki*
Roasted-Beet and Arugula Salad
Fennel and Roasted Red-Pepper Salad
Wild Greens and Cabbage Salad—*Hortosalata*
Roasted Cumin Carrots
Arugula and *Haloumi* Salad
Green Beans with Tomato—*Fasolakia*
Braised Cauliflower with Slowly Sautéed Onions
Broccoli Rabe with Garlic and White Cannellini Beans
Eggplant Casserole—A Simpler, Lighter *Moussaka*
Summer Vegetable Bake—*Briam*
Braised Kale with Red Peppers
Drunken Mushrooms
Caramelized Eggplant—*Imam Baildi*
Lemon and Oregano Roasted Potatoes—*Patates Fournou*
Okra and Tomatoes—*Bamies*
Stuffed Eggplant and Zucchini—*Papoutsakia*
Roasted Carrots with Rosemary and Sage
Sweet Potato, Zucchini, and Feta Tart
Zucchini and Tomatoes with Cumin and Caraway Seeds

SOME YEARS AGO two books were published that promoted the scientific evidence for eating a colorful variety of fruits and vegetables. *What Color Is Your Diet?* and *The Color Code: A Revolutionary Eating Plan for Optimum Health* shared the same premise: fruits and vegetables of different colors provide different phytochemicals that are required by our bodies to fight off disease and keeps us healthy.

COLOR AND VARIETY ARE ESSENTIAL

Instead of focusing just on consuming five or more servings of fruits and vegetables each day, both books asserted the benefits of eating a great variety of brightly colored produce daily. Here are a few of the reasons why.

Red tomatoes, watermelon, and pink grapefruit contain lycopene. Lycopene is best known for its beneficial effects on prostate health, but it is also known to protect the lungs and heart from oxidative harm.

Dark red, blue, and purple produce—such as strawberries, raspberries, blueberries, blackberries, cranberries, pomegranates, apples, grapes, plums, red onions, and eggplant—contain anthocyanins. Anthocyanins are antioxidants that protect us from oxidative stress that can cause heart disease. Studies have shown that antioxidants from fresh fruits and vegetables help keep us active and youthful in mind and body.

Carrots, sweet potatoes, butternut and acorn squash, pumpkins, cantaloupe, apricots, and other orange produce contain alpha- and beta-carotenes. Alpha-carotenes are thought to protect us from cancer while beta-carotenes protect our vision.

The all-important green vegetables—such as kale, broccoli, cabbage, brussels sprouts, spinach, and okra—contain lutein, which is essential for eye health and especially the prevention of macular degeneration. Green vegetables are also a source of a host of phytochemicals, such as sulforaphanes, other isothiocyanates, and indoles, which defend our bodies against cancer.

Even the pale green and white vegetables contribute to the arsenal of phytochemicals needed for optimal health. Members of the allium or onion family—such as garlic, onions, scallions, and leeks—contain allicin, which has antitumor properties. Yellow and red onions also contain quercetin, which is a flavonoid and helps fight cardiovascular disease by inhibiting the oxidation of LDL (bad) cholesterol. Flavonoids are also thought to be effective in controling one's weight, preventing cancer, and boosting the immune system. (Heber, *What Color Is Your Diet?;* Joseph, Nadeau, and Underwood, *The Color Code;* About.com: Cholesterol)

In addition, omega-3 fatty acids called alpha-linolenic, or ALA, are found in most dark-green leafy vegetables and legumes. These are necessary for brain health and help to provide the right balance of essential fatty acids associated with a lower risk for heart disease, cancer, diabetes, autoimmune diseases, and depression (Simopoulos and Robinson, *The Omega Diet,* 16, 28). In the traditional Greek diet, *horta,* or greens growing in the wild, are commonly consumed.

Homocysteine is an amino acid that, in high concentration, can damage the coronary arteries. It has been estimated to be responsible for 30 percent of the heart attacks and strokes affecting American men. Folic acid, a vitamin found in green leafy vegetables, legumes, and fruits, can reduce homocysteine levels (Simopoulos and Robinson, *The Omega Diet,* 50). We think of fresh fruits and vegetables as being a good source of dietary fiber, and they are. But until we consider the phytonutrients available to us through plant foods, we may take their importance for granted. Imagine how many more fruits and vegetables you would eat if you ate very little meat. Vegetables by the cup, especially in a rainbow of colors, were a mainstay in traditional Greek homes and should be at the forefront of this Greek Revival.

In the Mediterranean-cooking classes at the University of South Carolina's Cancer Prevention and Control Program, the vegetable class is the most popular. It features vegetarian main courses and side dishes. Depending on the season, the colorful bounty changes, but it has included red Swiss chard and beets; orange sweet potatoes, acorn squash, and carrots; green zucchini, spinach, and okra; purple eggplant; green leafy broccoli rabe and kale; and yellow summer squash and watermelon. Most students agree that they fall into the habit of buying and cooking the same few vegetables all the time. They enroll in the class, in part, to learn about vegetables with which they are less familiar. With the phytonutrient color wheel, it's easy to understand how choosing a variety of colors in vegetables can provide our bodies with the many nutrients we need. By expanding our vegetable repertoire we're investing in a variety of nutrients that are far more enjoyable to ingest than vitamin pills!

Growing one's own vegetables is satisfying in so many ways. By having control of the kinds of fertilizers and pesticides used, one can feel confident in the quality of the food consumed. It is also sheer pleasure to watch plants grow, flower, and bear fruit. What a sense of satisfaction! It's exciting to see more and more schools planting food gardens; in Vermont alone the Friends of Burlington Gardens & the Vermont Community Garden Network

Website (www.burlingtongardens.org/) lists more than sixty school gardens. The "edible landscape" movement is helping homeowners use even their front yards to create visually attractive vegetable gardens, and among city dwellers container gardening is becoming increasingly popular.

Community Supported Agriculture (CSA) is popping up all over the country, even in urban areas, where people can purchase a share in a farm's vegetable harvest and receive an allotment of freshly picked vegetables every week. Some groups are even operated like food cooperatives, where participants can opt to exchange physical labor on the farm for their vegetable allocation.

Local farm stands and farmers' markets are no longer found only in rural farming communities and hip cities. They are becoming more common in the suburbs, where there is mounting interest in locally grown produce.

To follow a traditional Greek diet, we need to increase our consumption of fresh fruits and vegetables by severalfold. Fortunately our opportunities to grow them ourselves or buy them locally are on the rise. By using color as a guide, we won't have to remember the multisyllabic names of all the phytonutrients, antioxidants, and flavonoids we will consume, but with that infusion of folic acid, we just might find we remember them all!

"NO DRINKING COFFEE AT YOUR DESK, . . .
BUT YOU'RE GONNA LOVE LUNCH"

By his third day of work at the University of Athens Medical School, my husband was no longer drinking coffee at his desk. The researchers took their midmorning coffee together at an appointed time, and they went to the cafeteria to drink it. It must have been something like the "coffee break" of generations ago in the United States. We might have gone to a work cafeteria to buy a coffee, but rarely in American professional circles did we sit together with colleagues, sip coffee, and visit. Many of our American associates even took lunch right at their desks, motoring through the workday.

Not so in Athens. With their coffee Harris's colleagues sat together for about thirty minutes before heading back to work. They talked about their families, weekend trips, politics, television—anything but work! Through these coffee breaks, relationships evolved. They had no need for "team building retreats." This social time was sacrosanct.

Lunch hour proved to be far more unusual. Harris started out bringing his lunch from home and eating it at about noon. No one else seemed interested in eating then. Instead, by the time he was finished eating, everyone around him had begun stacking up their work, turning off their computers, and leaving the office. To his surprise the office remained still from 1:30 P.M. until about 4:00 P.M. Then, as his energy was fading and he searched for coffee or better yet chocolate, his associates were returning to work refreshed, as if it were another morning. They had gone home, eaten their main meal of the day, and taken a nice siesta. Their workday ultimately ended at 8 P.M., and sometime in the evening they would enjoy a light supper.

In those days Dr. Dimitrios Trichopoulos was beginning research into the health benefits of this practice. In February 2007 he and his colleagues published a study in which participants were followed for six years. The results were encouraging; working men who enjoyed at least three thirty-minute or longer midday naps per week experienced a 37 percent lower coronary death rate than those who did not nap (Nasca and others, "Siesta in Healthy Adults").

Even before the scientific results were quantified, Harris decided to try it. For the first time in our lives, he came home for lunch. Thanks to the local farmers' market (*liaki*), we had kilos of colorful vegetables week after week. For lunch we ate caramelized oven-braised vegetable dishes, stuffed vegetables, fresh salads, crusty breads, and a glass or two of wine—when in Rome! Then we closed the vented metal shutters of our sliding glass doors to darken the room and fell into bed. With our two young children safe at school, it was a respite we got used to very quickly, a weekday retreat.

The anecdotal results of our midday napping "study": decreased stress, no heart symptoms (though we had none before), and a profound sense of serenity and happiness. The only negative result was a persistent disagreement concerning whose turn it was to get up to meet the school bus when we heard it grinding up the hill. Conclusion: More research is warranted . . . !

Greek Salad—*Salata Horiatiki*

2 ripe local tomatoes

1 ripe local cucumber

½ cup finely diced sweet
onion (approximately half
a medium-size onion)

½ cup sheep's milk feta
cheese, crumbled

½ cup kalamata olives

For dressing:

⅓ cup olive oil

1 tablespoon red-wine vinegar

1 tablespoon fresh-squeezed
lemon juice

1 teaspoon dried oregano

Sea salt and pepper to taste

WASH THE TOMATOES and remove the stem ends. Cut the tomatoes in half first, then slice them into ¾-inch-wide wedges. If the tomatoes are large, cut the wedges in half lengthwise.

Peel the cucumber and then slice it into ⅓ inch rounds. If the cucumber is very thick, cut the rounds in half.

Combine the tomato, cucumber, and diced onion in a bowl and add the crumbled feta cheese and kalamata olives. Toss to combine well.

In a small mixing bowl whisk the olive oil with the red-wine vinegar and lemon juice. Add dried oregano and sea salt and pepper to taste.

Pour the dressing over the salad, toss well, and serve immediately.

Serves 2–4

Cypriot Village Salad— *Salata Horiatiki*

WASH THE TOMATOES and remove the stem ends. Cut the tomatoes in half first, then slice them into ¾-inch wedges. If the tomatoes are large, cut the wedges in half.

Peel the cucumber and then slice it into ⅓-inch rounds. If the cucumber is very thick, cut the rounds in half.

Combine tomato, cucumber, onion, and cilantro in a bowl and set aside.

In a small mixing bowl whisk olive oil, red-wine vinegar, and lemon juice. Add sea salt and pepper to taste.

Pour the dressing over the salad, toss well, and serve immediately.

Serves 2–4

2 ripe local tomatoes

1 ripe local cucumber

¼ cup finely diced sweet onion

¼ cup washed, dried, and chopped cilantro leaves

For dressing:

⅓ cup olive oil

1 tablespoon red wine vinegar

1 tablespoon fresh-squeezed lemon juice

Sea salt and pepper to taste

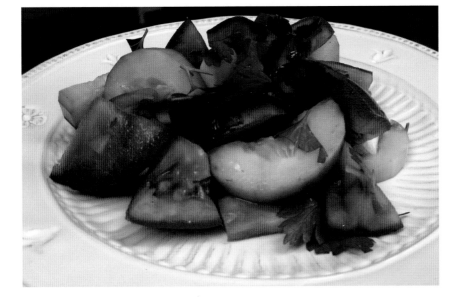

Roasted-Beet and Arugula Salad

As with most vegetables, roasting brings out the sweetness of beets, which are delicious when paired with the peppery taste of arugula. With just a hint of licorice flavor, fennel seed adds a nice touch.

PREHEAT THE OVEN to 400 degrees.

Wash and peel the beets and cut off the greens. (If the greens are fresh, reserve them to make Onion and Beet-Green *Pita,* page 24.)

Cut each beet in half and then into ½–¾-inch wedges. Place the beet wedges on a small cookie sheet and set aside.

In a small mixing bowl, combine 3 tablespoons of olive oil, 2 teaspoons of Dijon mustard, ¼ cup of orange juice, and ½ teaspoon of dried fennel seed. Stir or whisk well and pour this marinade over the beet wedges, tossing until the beets are completely coated. Cook the beets uncovered in a 400-degree oven for approximately 30 minutes or until they are tender. If you are using a conventional oven, turn the beets over once after about 15 minutes so they will cook evenly. If you are using a convection oven, you may not need to turn the beets at all.

Remove the beets from the oven and let them cool.

In a medium-size frying pan, heat 1 tablespoon of olive oil. Add the almonds and toss to coat in oil. Cook over medium-high heat for a few minutes, shaking the pan occasionally, until the almonds darken to a deeper brown. Remove the pan from the heat and set aside.

Roughly chop the arugula and put it in a large mixing bowl.

Prepare the Dijon vinaigrette by whisking ½ cup of olive oil, 3 tablespoons of balsamic vinegar, and 1 teaspoon of Dijon mustard until thoroughly combined. Pour this vinaigrette over the arugula and toss to coat.

Peel the orange, cut it into small pieces, and remove the seeds.

On each individual salad plate, place a portion of arugula in the center, then artfully arrange the beets and pieces of orange around the plate. Top with toasted almonds.

Serves 4–6

For roasting beets:

2 large beets
3 tablespoons olive oil
2 teaspoons Dijon mustard
¼ cup orange juice
½ teaspoon dried fennel seed

For preparing almonds and arugula:

1 tablespoon olive oil
⅔ cup raw almonds
4 cups arugula, washed
 and dried

For Dijon vinaigrette:

½ cup olive oil
3 tablespoons balsamic
 vinegar
1 teaspoon Dijon mustard

1 Minneola orange for garnish

For a pleasant variation use hazelnut vinegar and omit the mustard in the vinaigrette.

Fennel and Roasted Red-Pepper Salad

1 bulb fennel

¼ cup olive oil

2 tablespoons fresh-squeezed lemon juice

Sea salt and pepper to taste

¼ teaspoon caraway seeds

1 roasted red pepper (see page 15), sliced into very thin strips

4–8 pieces shaved Parmesan cheese

Fennel fronds for garnish

CUT THE FRONDS from the fennel bulb and set aside. Wash and core the fennel bulb and discard the hard core. Slice the bulb into very thin strips and place them in a medium-size mixing bowl.

In a small mixing bowl, whisk together the olive oil, lemon juice, sea salt and pepper, and caraway seeds.

Pour this dressing over the fennel and toss well to coat.

Divide the fennel among four salad plates and set aside.

Slice the roasted red pepper into very thin strips and divide it equally among the four salad plates, placing it on top of the fennel. Top each salad with 1–2 pieces of shaved Parmesan cheese.

Chop the fennel fronds into small pieces and sprinkle over salads as a garnish.

Serve immediately.

Serves 4

Wild Greens and Cabbage Salad—*Hortosalata*

In Greece wild greens (*horto*) are harvested from the hillsides, boiled until very soft, and served with olive oil and lemon juice or vinegar and sea salt. This salad comprises the "wilder" side of cultivated lettuces, which are tender enough to eat raw. The cabbage and the radishes contribute the crunch. The lemon juice in the dressing is reminiscent of traditional *horta*.

WASH AND ROUGHLY CHOP a mixture of "wild" greens such as dandelion, mustard, arugula, purslane, and sorrel. The young leaves of these plants are tender and suitable for salad. Cut the cabbage into thin slices, and then cut the slices in half, so they are no longer than 2–3 inches. Wash and chop five radishes into small wedges.

Toss the greens, cabbage, and radishes into a large salad bowl and set aside. Make the salad dressing by whisking the olive oil, lemon juice, dried oregano, and sea salt and pepper to taste in a small pitcher.

Just before serving, whisk the dressing again and pour it over the salad. Garnish with whole radishes.

Serves 8

5 cups wild greens
3 cups cabbage
  (approximately ¼
  medium cabbage)
5 radishes

For dressing:
¾ cup olive oil
¼ cup fresh lemon juice
½ teaspoon dried oregano
Sea salt and pepper

2 small radishes for garnish

Roasted Cumin Carrots

15 whole large carrots (approximately 8 inches long)

⅓ cup olive oil

⅓ cup orange juice

1 teaspoon balsamic vinegar

1 tablespoon ground cumin

½ cup water

1 sprig fresh oregano for garnish

PREHEAT THE OVEN to 375 degrees.

Cut the stems and tips from the whole carrots and discard. Peel the carrots and score them by slicing partway into them shallowly on a diagonal, concentrating on the thickest parts. Spread the carrots out on a baking sheet leaving some space between them.

In a large measuring cup or a small mixing bowl, combine the olive oil, orange juice, balsamic vinegar, and ground cumin. Whisk well to combine. Pour the mixture over the carrots and roll them in the marinade to coat all sides.

Place the baking sheet in the oven and roast for a total of 45 minutes. About halfway through the cooking time, the liquid will have evaporated, so pour ½ cup of water over the carrots and cook the remainder of the time until they have browned and are fork tender.

Transfer Roasted Cumin Carrots to a serving dish and garnish with a sprig of fresh oregano.

Serves 6 as a side dish

Arugula and *Haloumi* Salad

1 block imported *haloumi*
cheese (about 11 ounces)

1 teaspoon olive oil

4 cups fresh arugula leaves

For dressing:

½ cup olive oil

2 tablespoons red-wine
vinegar

2 tablespoons fresh-squeezed
lemon juice

Sea salt and pepper

SLICE *haloumi* lengthwise into ⅓-inch slices. Heat 1 teaspoon olive oil over medium-high heat in a frying pan. Place *haloumi* in the moderately hot pan and fry for a few minutes. If the oil begins to smoke, lower the heat a bit. Don't turn the cheese until it feels firm. Carefully check by lifting one piece with tongs to see if the pan side has browned. When the pan side is brown, carefully turn each piece and fry the other side. The *haloumi* will become a beautiful golden brown on both sides and will remain firm. When all the *haloumi* is browned, remove it from the heat and set it aside.

Roughly chop the arugula leaves to release the flavor. Place the leaves in a large salad bowl and set aside.

Make the dressing by whisking together the olive oil, red-wine vinegar, lemon juice, a bit of sea salt, and freshly ground black pepper.

Pour the dressing over the arugula and toss well to coat. Divide the arugula among individual salad plates.

Place 1 or 2 pieces of *haloumi* on each salad and serve immediately.

Serves 4–6

Green Beans with Tomato—
Fasolakia

AT MEDIUM TEMPERATURE, heat 2 tablespoons of olive oil in a large sauté pan and gently sauté the sliced onion and garlic until they are soft and beginning to brown. Add the green beans and sea salt and pepper to taste. Cover and cook for 15 minutes over medium-low heat. Add the finely chopped tomatoes, red wine, and oregano. Cover and cook until the beans are very soft. Cooking time will vary between 20 to 30 minutes depending on the thickness of your beans.

This dish may be enjoyed immediately or at room temperature.

Serves 4 as a side dish

2 tablespoons olive oil

1 large onion, sliced thinly

1 clove garlic, sliced thinly

¾ pound green beans, trimmed

Sea salt and pepper

3 tomatoes, chopped finely

¼ cup red wine

¼ teaspoon dried oregano

Braised Cauliflower with Slowly Sautéed Onions

With their sweetness, slowly sautéed onions enhance the flavor of just about anything. In this recipe the textures play as big a role as the flavors. The cauliflower is tender but not mushy, and the onions are silky. The fresh herbs provide a deep, savory flavor and add a lovely green color.

IN A LARGE SAUTÉ PAN, heat ¼ cup of olive oil over medium-high heat. Add all the sliced onions, stir to coat with oil, and lower the heat to medium. Sauté the onions for approximately 30 minutes until they are completely soft and beginning to turn light brown. Stir in the chopped oregano and sage leaves and cook for a few more minutes. The onions should be a uniform brown, and the herbs should be wilted. Remove the pan from the heat and transfer the contents to a large serving bowl. Add sea salt and pepper to taste.

Using the same large sauté pan, heat 3 tablespoons of olive oil over medium-high heat. Add the pieces of cauliflower and stir to coat them with oil, cooking for a few minutes while stirring. The cauliflower will begin to brown. Cover the pan and lower the heat to medium low. Let the cauliflower cook this way for a few more minutes. Take off the lid and stir again. The cauliflower should be tender but not soft. Pour the white wine over the cauliflower, add sea salt and pepper, raise the heat to medium high, and stir. Cook, stirring occasionally, until the wine evaporates. Remove the pan from the heat. Add the cauliflower to the onions and stir gently to combine.

Garnish the serving bowl with the sprigs of fresh oregano.

Serve Braised Cauliflower with Slowly Sautéed Onions over brown rice.

Serves 6–8

¼ cup olive oil
4 medium onions, thinly sliced (approximately 4 cups)
¼ cup chopped fresh oregano leaves
⅓ cup chopped fresh sage leaves
Sea salt and pepper

3 tablespoons olive oil
1 large head cauliflower cut into 2-inch pieces (approximately 6 cups)
⅔ cup dry white wine

Sprigs of fresh oregano for garnish

Broccoli Rabe with Garlic and White Cannellini Beans

This is a wonderful, tasty side dish to accompany any meal. It goes well with a menu that needs a flavorful vegetable dish. Most meat-centered meals are enhanced by the addition of a garlicky side dish, and with Broccoli Rabe with Garlic and White Cannellini Beans, you have the benefit of a dark-green leafy vegetable combined with fibrous and filling beans, encouraging the diner to consume a smaller portion of meat. Traditional Greek-style meals comprise six or seven dishes, many of which are vegetable or grain side dishes. Even when meat is served, diners don't tend to eat large portions of it.

Canned beans are certainly convenient, but compare the labels to be sure the canned beans you choose contain the lowest amount of sodium.

1 large bunch broccoli rabe

3 tablespoons olive oil

6 cloves garlic, minced

1 15-ounce can white cannellini beans, strained and liquid discarded

Red-pepper flakes

Sea salt

Asiago cheese, grated

PREPARE THE BROCCOLI RABE by washing it thoroughly and cutting away the thick stems. Chop the leaves and the thin stems into small pieces and dry them in a salad spinner. It is important to dry the broccoli rabe as much as possible to minimize splattering when it hits the hot oil.

Heat the olive oil in a large sauté pan over medium heat and gently sauté the minced garlic until it becomes light brown. Be careful not to burn the garlic because it will create a bitter flavor.

Add half the broccoli rabe to the sauté pan and stir. Cook until the greens wilt a bit and shrink, creating space for the remainder of the broccoli rabe to be added to the pan.

Add the second half of broccoli rabe and cook, stirring occasionally, until it has turned a uniform bright-green color and is wilted.

Add the strained cannellini beans and stir to combine. Sprinkle with red-pepper flakes and sea salt to taste.

Turn off the heat and place the Broccoli Rabe with Garlic and White Cannellini Beans in a serving dish.

Sprinkle with grated Asiago cheese and serve immediately.

Serves 4–6

Eggplant Casserole— A Simpler, Lighter *Moussaka*

Traditional *moussaka* is made by frying slices of eggplant and potato, layering them with a savory meat sauce, and then topping the casserole with a cheesy béchamel sauce. My Traditional *Moussaka* recipe on page 157 is somewhat lighter as the eggplant and potato slices are brushed with olive oil and broiled so they don't absorb as much oil. I also use a lean cut of beef and low-fat milk in the béchamel sauce.

The following recipe is even lighter as a simple tomato-onion sauce is substituted for the meat sauce and a sprinkle of grated cheese replaces the béchamel sauce—rendering this recipe simpler and lighter.

WASH, TRIM, AND SLICE the eggplants lengthwise into ¼-inch slices.

Salt each slice and layer them all in a large colander to drain. Put a heavy plate on top of the eggplant. The salt and the weight of the plate will accelerate the draining of excess water from the eggplant. Let the slices drain at least 30 minutes. Dry eggplant slices with a clean kitchen towel.

Brush both sides of each slice of eggplant lightly with olive oil.

Place the slices of eggplant under the broiler and brown them thoroughly. When one side is brown, turn them over, and brown the other side.

Add sea salt and pepper to taste and set aside.

Preheat the oven to 350 degrees.

In a large sauté pan over medium heat, heat 2 tablespoons of olive oil; add the chopped onions and garlic and sauté until the onions are translucent. Add the crushed tomatoes and ¼ cup of the white wine and cook for 15 minutes on low heat until the sauce is reduced. It should not be completely dry, but most of the liquid should have evaporated.

Remove from heat and place half the tomato sauce in the bottom of a medium-size casserole dish (such as 9-inch square).

Layer half the eggplant on top of the sauce and sprinkle with ¼ cup of cheese.

Top with the remaining eggplant, sauce, and cheese. Pour the remaining ¼ cup of white wine around the edges of the casserole. Cover and bake for 30 minutes. Uncover and bake for 5 additional minutes.

For peak flavor serve at room temperature.

Serves 4–6 as a main dish

4 small eggplants
Sea salt
¼ cup plus 2 tablespoons olive oil
Black pepper
2 medium-size yellow onions, chopped
2 cloves garlic, crushed and chopped
1½ cups crushed tomato (canned crushed tomatoes work well)
½ cup dry white wine
½ cup grated *kefalotiri* cheese (may substitute Parmesan or Romano)

Kefalotiri *is a very hard, salty, and sharp cheese made from a combination of sheep's milk and goat's milk. It is used for grating over food and is similar to Parmesan, Asiago, and Romano cheeses.*

Summer Vegetable Bake— *Briam*

I found *briam* on several menus in Cyprus and discovered that the term means different things to different chefs. The basic concept is to create an oven-baked casserole from a mélange of vegetables, usually with some cheese.

This version is appealing because the vegetables are thinly sliced and layered, so instead of eating one chunk of a vegetable at a time, you get to taste them together, which I find far more interesting.

3 large potatoes

2 zucchini

2 yellow summer squash

5 tablespoons olive oil

¾ pound strained ricotta cheese (part skim is fine)

15–18 mint leaves, washed, dried and chopped

3 large tomatoes

Sea salt and pepper

PREHEAT THE OVEN to 375 degrees.

Prepare all the vegetables by slicing them as thinly as possible. (A mandolin is very handy for this recipe.)

Pour 2 tablespoons of olive oil in bottom of a 9 x 11-inch baking dish and rub to coat the bottom and sides of the pan. Place one layer of sliced potato, then one layer of sliced zucchini. Drizzle a little olive oil on top. Beat the ricotta cheese with a fork and drop half of the cheese by spoonfuls on top of the zucchini. Spread the ricotta cheese on the zucchini with a spatula. Sprinkle with sea salt and pepper and half of the chopped mint.

Next layer more sliced potato followed by the summer squash. Drizzle 1 tablespoon of olive oil over the squash and sprinkle with sea salt and pepper. Top with the remaining cheese and mint. Finish by layering sliced tomatoes in overlapping rows on top of the casserole. Drizzle with the final tablespoon of olive oil and sea salt and pepper again.

The olive oil allows the vegetables to soften without drying and to crisp around the edges when uncovered. The sea salt, pepper, and olive oil together enhance the wonderful flavors of the vegetables.

Cover with foil and bake in the oven until all the vegetables are soft, approximately 2 hours. The foil should be removed for the last 30 minutes so the vegetables can caramelize.

May be served warm or at room temperature.

Serves 6 as main dish or 8 as side dish

Braised Kale with Red Peppers

If you avoid greens because you don't relish the soggy texture of boiled greens, try these. In Braised Kale with Red Peppers, the oven braising makes the kale very soft, but not soggy, and crispy on the edges.

PREHEAT THE OVEN to 400 degrees.

Wash the kale and rough chop the leaves, discarding any thick stems. Set aside.

Core and slice the red peppers into 1-inch-wide strips. Peel the clove of garlic and slice it thinly. Put the strips of red peppers, chopped kale, and slices of garlic in a medium-size roasting pan and stir to combine. Pour the olive oil over the vegetables and sprinkle with sea salt and pepper.

Cook uncovered in the oven, stirring occasionally, for about 20 minutes. Pour the red wine over the vegetables and stir. Cook for another 10 minutes until the peppers are soft and the greens are very wilted and browned on the edges.

Serve warm from the oven.

Serves 4–6 as a side dish

1 large bowl of kale leaves
(approximately 8 cups
when chopped)
2 red bell peppers
1 large clove garlic
⅓ cup olive oil
Sea salt and pepper
½ cup red wine

Drunken Mushrooms

12–14 large white mushrooms, washed, trimmed, and quartered

1 clove garlic, minced

1 tablespoon plus 1 teaspoon olive oil

1 teaspoon coriander seeds, crushed with a mortar and pestle

Black pepper in grinder

Slight sprinkle of cayenne pepper (less than $\frac{1}{8}$ teaspoon)

$\frac{3}{4}$ cup dry red wine

Sea salt

$\frac{1}{4}$ cup small basil leaves

HEAT 1 TABLESPOON of olive oil in a medium-size sauté pan over medium heat. Add minced garlic and gently sauté. Add crushed coriander seeds and stir with a wooden spoon. Cook for a few minutes to release the flavor.

Turn up the temperature to medium high and add the mushrooms to the hot pan. Stir to blend all the ingredients.

Add 10–12 turns of cracked black pepper and a very light sprinkle of cayenne pepper (less than $\frac{1}{8}$ teaspoon). Lightly sprinkle with sea salt and then cover in red wine.

Simmer until all the red wine is absorbed, approximately 15–20 minutes, stirring occasionally.

Remove the pan from the heat and spoon the mushrooms into a serving dish.

Heat 1 teaspoon of olive oil in a small frying pan over medium-high heat. Add basil leaves and cook 2–3 minutes, turning once.

Remove from the heat, salt lightly, and add to the mushrooms.

Drunken Mushrooms may be served hot or at room temperature. They are an especially savory accompaniment to any dinner featuring a meat dish.

Serves 4–6 as a side dish

Caramelized Eggplant— *Imam Baildi*

I found the most wonderful tiny eggplants from a local farmer. They were a royal-purple color, and none was larger than a tennis ball. Some were comparable in size to golf balls! The *imam baildi* photograph shows you just how precious they were. These are the ultimate eggplants for the perfect *imam baildi,* which—by the way—translates as "the imam fainted" (presumably from tasting this luscious dish)!

With tiny eggplants:

25 tiny eggplants, washed and trimmed

2 teaspoons sea salt for soaking eggplant

⅓ cup olive oil, plus 1–2 tablespoons for bottom of pan

3 cups diced Vidalia onions

5 cloves garlic, minced

3 cups crushed tomatoes (canned or grated fresh tomatoes)

1½ cups diced tomatoes (if canned, strain off liquid)

1 scant teaspoon sugar

1 teaspoon sea salt

½ teaspoon black pepper

1 tablespoon olive oil

4 tablespoons pine nuts

18 fresh whole basil leaves

WITH TINY EGGPLANTS:

If you find tiny eggplants the size of a tennis ball and smaller, here are the proportions of ingredients to use.

Follow the main recipe directions below, but with these tiny eggplants, just cut slits into them, rather than cutting them into pieces. These firm eggplants took 70 minutes to cook in a 400-degree oven. They were covered for the first 30 minutes and uncovered for the last 40 minutes. I checked them a couple of times, and turned them while they cooked. They were amazing!

MAIN RECIPE:

Cut the eggplants lengthwise to make large wedges, approximately 1–1½ inches thick. If the eggplant wedges are more than 5 inches long, cut them in half to make shorter pieces approximately the same size.

In a bowl large enough to hold all the eggplant, soak it in salted water (with 2 teaspoons of sea salt) for 30 minutes. Use a heavy plate to keep the eggplant submerged.

Heat the larger quantity of olive oil in a medium frying pan over medium-high heat, add the onions to the pan, stir to cover in oil, lower the heat to medium, and sauté the diced onions until soft and golden. Add the minced garlic and cook for a minute or two, stirring with the onions. Add all the tomatoes and the sugar, sea salt, and black pepper.

Turn up the heat, bringing the mixture to a gentle boil, then lower the heat and simmer for 10 minutes while stirring with a wooden spoon. If you are using fresh tomatoes, you may need to cook them longer. Fresh tomatoes should be soft, and the tomato juice should be reduced by about half. Remove from the heat and set aside.

Preheat the oven to 400 degrees.

Prepare a heavy casserole dish with a lid by drizzling the bottom with 1–2 tablespoons of olive oil. Remove the eggplant from the salted water and squeeze gently. Place the eggplant wedges in the bottom of the casserole dish and cover with the tomato/onion mixture. Cover the casserole dish and place it in the center of the oven.

The goal of this recipe is to cook the eggplant long enough so that all the natural moisture has escaped and evaporated. The only liquid left in the casserole should be olive oil. The eggplant, tomato, and onion should all taste richly pungent, and the texture should be very soft.

Baking time depends largely on the density of the eggplants. Generally you should expect this recipe to bake for at least 1½–2 hours. To achieve soft caramelized eggplant, start by cooking the casserole covered for the first 45 minutes, then uncover it and cook for at least another 45 minutes.

When the eggplant is fully cooked, remove the pan from the oven and let it stand uncovered. This dish is most flavorful served slightly warm. You may cook it ahead of time and reheat it just before serving.

When you are ready to serve the *imam baildi,* heat 1 tablespoon of olive oil in a small frying pan and toast the pine nuts. Turn them with a wooden spoon continually to brown the nuts evenly. When the pine nuts are light brown, toss in the basil leaves and sauté these for a minute or two.

Transfer the *imam baildi* to a serving dish and garnish with the toasted pine nuts and basil leaves.

Serves 6–8 (tiny eggplant recipe) or 4–6 (small eggplant recipe) as a main dish.

Main recipe:

4 small eggplants (each about the size of a softball), washed and trimmed

2 teaspoons sea salt for soaking eggplant

¼ cup olive oil, plus 1–2 tablespoons for bottom of pan

2 cups diced Vidalia onions

3 cloves garlic, minced

1½ cups crushed tomatoes (canned or grated fresh tomatoes)

1 cup diced tomatoes (if using canned diced tomatoes, strain off the liquid)

½ teaspoon sugar

½ teaspoon sea salt

¼ teaspoon black pepper

1 tablespoon olive oil

2 tablespoons pine nuts

10–12 fresh, whole basil leaves

Lemon and Oregano Roasted Potatoes—*Patates Fournou*

PREHEAT THE OVEN to 400 degrees.

Wash and quarter the red potatoes. If they are large (the size of a baseball), cut them in half first, then quarter the halves. Try to cut them so all the pieces are of a similar size. Place the potatoes on a heavy baking sheet. Pour the olive oil over the potatoes and toss to thoroughly coat. (I like to use my hands to be certain that all sides of the potatoes are coated with oil.) Sprinkle the juice of one lemon over the potatoes, and then sprinkle them evenly with oregano.

Bake for 30 minutes. Turn the potatoes and sprinkle them with the juice of half a lemon. Bake for another 30 minutes until the potatoes are golden brown. Remove from the heat and sprinkle with the juice of half a lemon. Sprinkle sea salt on the potatoes to taste and spoon them into a serving dish.

This recipe is best served right from the oven.

Serves 6–8 as a side dish

12 medium-size red potatoes
$\frac{1}{4}$ cup olive oil
2 tablespoons dried oregano
Juice of 2 lemons
Sea salt

Never salt potatoes until they are done because the salt will draw water from the potatoes as they are cooking, leaving them soggy and sticking to the pan.

Okra and Tomatoes— *Bamies*

Most people who don't like okra don't like it because it can be glutinous. If the okra stays whole during cooking and is not overcooked, you can avoid this "problem." (I use quotation marks here because some people enjoy the texture.)

Okra is very popular in Cyprus, and stewing it with tomatoes is typical there. The following recipe starts by sautéing them whole, then finishes by braising them in the juice of fresh tomatoes. As you read the recipe you'll see the word *gently* more than once. To avoid viscosity it is critical not to pierce the flesh of the okra.

1 pound small okra (about 3 inches long)

¼ cup olive oil

2 medium yellow onions, chopped

4 large local tomatoes, chopped (or 2 14½-ounce cans of diced tomatoes strained, excess juice discarded)

1 clove garlic, crushed

1 tablespoon fresh lemon juice

½ teaspoon sea salt

¼ teaspoon black pepper

1 scant teaspoon sugar

Finely chopped fresh mint or basil for garnish

IN PREPARING THE OKRA, do not puncture the flesh. Cut off the stems leaving a bit of stem attached so that the okra will remain whole. Wash and dry the trimmed okra.

In a large sauté pan, heat the olive oil over medium heat and add the chopped onions to the pan. Slowly sauté the onions, stirring occasionally, until they are soft and golden. Add the okra and, using a wooden spoon, gently toss the okra carefully to combine them with the onions. Let the okra and onions cook over medium heat for about 10 minutes.

Add the chopped tomatoes, garlic, lemon juice, sea salt, pepper, and sugar. Stir gently to blend the seasonings and then cover the pan and simmer for 10 minutes. Uncover the pan and cook for another 10 minutes to reduce the liquid from the tomatoes. If you are using fresh tomatoes you may need to increase the cooking time as fresh tomatoes can be very juicy. The okra should be tender, and there should be very little "sauce" left in the pan.

Transfer the *bamies* to a serving dish and garnish with finely chopped fresh mint or basil leaves.

Bamies may be served immediately or at room temperature. It may be used as a hearty side dish, but it is very often served in small portions as an appetizer (*mezedakia*).

Serve 6–8 as a side dish

If you have very small tender okra (under 3 inches in length and thin) you may need to cook them with the onions for only 5 minutes before proceeding with the recipe.

Stuffed Eggplant and Zucchini—*Papoutsakia*

Papoutsakia is a Greek word meaning "little shoes." In this recipe we stuff little eggplants and zucchini as if they were little shoes. This luscious vegetable dish is a very typical Greek slow-cooked creation. Patience brings the vegetables to their most succulent caramelized softness, and an extra drizzle of olive oil never hurts!

6 tiny eggplants, washed

6 small, thin zucchini, washed

2 teaspoons sea salt for soaking eggplant

¼ cup olive oil and an additional 1–2 tablespoons to drizzle

2 medium yellow onions, diced small

3 cloves garlic, minced

3 cups crushed tomatoes (canned or grated fresh tomatoes)

6 cups baby spinach, chopped

Sea salt

Black pepper

Red-pepper flakes

1–2 tablespoons olive oil

10–12 fresh basil leaves (whole, stems removed)

2 tablespoons pine nuts

DO NOT CUT OFF THE STEMS or bottoms of the vegetables. Cut each eggplant in half lengthwise and do the same with the zucchini. Scoop out the central flesh of the vegetables, leaving a ½-inch-thick shell. Chop the central flesh of the vegetables into small pieces and set aside.

In a bowl large enough to hold the eggplants, soak them in salted water (using 2 teaspoons of sea salt and water to cover the eggplant halves) for 30 minutes. Place a heavy plate on top to keep the eggplants submerged.

Heat ¼ cup of olive oil in a medium sauté pan over medium heat and sauté the onions until they are soft and golden. Add the minced garlic, stirring while it cooks for a few minutes so it doesn't burn. Add the chopped zucchini and eggplant and cook for a few minutes while stirring. Then add the crushed tomatoes and stir to combine. Turn up the heat and bring the mixture to a gentle boil, then lower the heat and simmer for approximately 10 minutes while stirring with a wooden spoon. Add the chopped spinach and stir until it is wilted and well combined with the tomato mixture. Add a sprinkle of sea salt and black pepper and red-pepper flakes to taste. Cook until the liquid is reduced by about half. Remove from the heat and let this stuffing mixture cool a bit.

Preheat the oven to 375 degrees.

Prepare a covered baking dish by brushing the bottom with 1–2 tablespoons of olive oil.

Remove the eggplant halves from the salted water and pat them dry with a clean kitchen towel. Place the eggplant and zucchini halves in the baking pan and fill them with the tomato/spinach/eggplant/zucchini/onion mixture.

Baking time depends largely on the size of the eggplants and zucchini. Plan on about 1½ hours. When done, the eggplants and zucchini should be thoroughly soft. To achieve soft caramelized *papoutsakia,* cook covered for the first 30 minutes, then uncover and drizzle with a little olive oil. Check the eggplants and zucchini periodically. If they look dry but are not yet soft, add a little water to the pan and cook until the vegetables are very soft and the water has evaporated. The *papoutsakia* should be almost to the point of falling apart.

Remove the casserole from the oven and let it stand. This dish is most flavorful at room temperature, but it may be served warm if you prefer.

When the dish is ready to serve, heat 1 tablespoon of olive oil in a small frying pan over medium heat and add the pine nuts. Turn the pine nuts with a wooden spoon continually to brown them evenly. When the pine nuts are light brown, toss in the basil leaves and sauté them for a minute or two.

Garnish *papoutsakia* with pine nuts and basil leaves.

Serves 6 as a main dish

This dish is exceptional if you can find very small purple eggplants about the size of small avocados.

Roasted Carrots with Rosemary and Sage

18 medium-size carrots

2–3 tablespoons olive oil

2 6-inch stems of fresh rosemary

10 fresh sage leaves

Sea salt

PREHEAT THE OVEN to 400 degrees.

Peel the carrots and trim their ends. Discard the ends. Unless they are very thin, slice carrots lengthwise. Very thin carrots can be roasted whole. They should be of uniform size.

Place the carrots on a heavy baking sheet and pour the olive oil over them. Using your hands, rub the oil onto all sides of the carrots to coat them thoroughly.

On a cutting board, use a knife to scrape the rosemary leaves from the stems. Discard the stems and chop the leaves to release the flavor. Sprinkle the chopped rosemary leaves over the carrots.

Wash and dry the sage leaves. Remove any long stems and discard them. Stack the leaves and roll them into a thin tube. Chiffonade the leaves by chopping finely from one end of the tube to the other. Sprinkle the sage "ribbons" over the carrots evenly.

Place the baking sheet in the center of the oven and roast the carrots for 50 minutes to 1 hour, turning once at 25–30 minutes. Roasting time will vary depending on the thickness of the carrots.

Carrots are best when they are browned on all sides and soft.

Remove the roasted carrots from the oven and sprinkle with sea salt.

Serve immediately.

Serves 4–6 as a side dish

Sweet Potato, Zucchini, and Feta Tart

1–2 tablespoons olive oil to prepare the baking dish

1 large sweet potato

2 medium zucchini

8 ounces sheep's milk feta cheese, crumbled

½ cup fresh basil leaves, finely chopped

1 teaspoon dried oregano

2 eggs

2 cups milk (1 percent works well)

2 tablespoons flour

1 teaspoon sea salt

¼ teaspoon pepper

PREHEAT THE OVEN to 375 degrees.

Oil the bottom and sides of a 9 x 11-inch baking dish. Grate the sweet potato and zucchini in a food processor or by using the large-holed side of a box grater. You should have approximately 2–3 cups of each. Stir grated sweet potato and zucchini together to blend and spread in the bottom of the baking dish. In a medium-size bowl, fold the basil and dried oregano into the crumbled feta cheese to combine. Sprinkle the cheese mixture evenly over the sweet potato and zucchini mixture.

In a blender or electric mixer, beat together the eggs, milk, flour, sea salt, and pepper. Pour the egg mixture over the top of the contents of the baking dish.

Bake for approximately 1 hour or until well set and slightly browned on top.

This tart is best served warm.

Serves 9 as a side dish

Zucchini and Tomatoes with Cumin and Caraway Seeds

In reading *Ancient Herbs* by Marina Heilmeyer, I learned that the flavors of cumin and caraway seeds were enjoyed together during ancient times. Since I've always liked caraway seeds, I thought I would try combining them with cumin in a vegetable dish. Zucchini was plentiful from the garden, so it became a likely candidate for the experiment. The result is tasty and unexpected; the cumin and caraway flavors complement the zucchini and tomatoes well. Just two spices give this standard dish a whole new zing!

IN A LARGE SAUCEPAN over medium heat, sauté the onions in the olive oil until they begin to soften. Add the chopped tomatoes to the pan and cook for a few minutes. Then add the cumin and caraway seeds and cook uncovered for a few minutes, stirring to combine the spices, tomatoes, and onions.

Add the thin slices of zucchini to the pan and cook over medium-high heat until the zucchini slices are soft and much of the juice from the tomatoes has evaporated. Add sea salt and pepper to taste.

In a dry sauté pan, toast the pine nuts over medium heat quickly, just until they turn golden.

Top the vegetables with the toasted pine nuts.

Serves 6

3 tablespoons olive oil

1 Vidalia onion, finely chopped

4 ripe local tomatoes, chopped

2 teaspoons cumin

2 teaspoons caraway seeds

3 small zucchini, sliced very thinly

Sea salt and pepper to taste

¼ cup pine nuts

Acorn-Squash and Ginger Soup
with Chickpeas, p. 95

3. BEANS, GRAINS, AND PASTA

◼

Bulgur and Bright Lentils
Lentil and Tomato Soup with Coriander and Cumin—*Fakies*
Fruited Chickpeas with Brown Rice
Spinach and Brown Rice—*Spanakorizo*
Pasta with Arugula, Tomatoes, Feta, and Kalamata Olives
Acorn-Squash and Ginger Soup with Chickpeas
Cabbage and Apple Bulgur
Vegetables Stuffed with Barley—*Gemista*
Gingered Brown Rice with Raisins and Orange
Sautéed Broccoli Rabe with Penne Pasta
Lima Bean and Carrot Soup—*Gigantes*
Black-Eyed Peas and Swiss Chard—*Lahana me Louvia*

A CENTRAL FEATURE of the traditional Mediterranean diet is that proteins are primarily derived from plant sources, including legumes and whole grains, as well as from a variety of seafood. Proteins from other animal sources are limited, though none is completely eliminated.

NUTRIENT-RICH PROTEINS AND COMPLEX CARBOHYDRATES

Complex carbohydrates, the slower-burning variety, are generally "nutrient dense," packed with a wide variety of vitamins, minerals, antioxidants, folates, and fiber—all of which add to the total nutritional value of the foods. Complex carbohydrates are typically consumed in their natural form. They are usually whole unprocessed foods such as fruits, vegetables, whole grains, and cereals. These "good carbs" minimize spikes in blood sugar, keep you feeling full longer, and provide nutrient-rich energy for the body.

Lentils are used in many traditional Greek recipes. They are convenient because they do not require soaking, and they cook quickly. They are a good source of protein and folates for preserving brain matter and healthy arteries, and they provide fiber for colon health and cholesterol management. They contain essential minerals and vitamins—and no fat. As with all legumes, lentils provide fuel for the body while they stabilize blood sugar.

When cooking lentils and beans, allow the liquid to boil *before* adding the legumes. This method purportedly eases digestion.

Lentils have been consumed since prehistoric times. Seeds found at archaeological sites have been dated back eight thousand years ("Lentils," The World's Healthiest Foods). Lentils are a valuable food to classify as part of a Greek Revival!

Dried lima beans, which are used for *gigantes* (Lima Bean and Carrot Soup, page 104), do need to be soaked before cooking. Leave your bag of beans on the counter if you need a reminder. Limas have many of the same nutritional qualities as the tiny lentils, but they stand up to longer cooking with larger chunks of carrots and create a nice thick soup on their own with a little tomato paste. Don't make the mistake of salting the water that you use to cook your lima beans. Salted water makes beans tough. The finishing touch for the *gigantes* is lots of fresh-squeezed lemon juice, which give this hearty bean soup a fresh zing.

Best of all, *gigantes* is another dish that is satisfying and filling. It tastes great and feeds the body with nutrients. When coupled with a whole grain, it provides a complete protein. In addition the magnesium in the limas encourages not only blood circulation but also the flow of oxygen and nutrients throughout the body. ("Lima beans," The World's Healthiest Foods). Limas are a true heart-healthy food, and again they contain no saturated fat and lots of fiber and nutrients.

Chickpeas provide a healthy source of protein in the Acorn-Squash and Ginger Soup with Chickpeas recipe (page 95). They are also a good source of dietary fiber, which contributes to lowering cholesterol and managing blood sugar. Chickpeas may be easily added to any grain recipe, such as Cabbage and Apple Bulgur (page 96) to create a dish that is a healthy substitute for a meat-based meal.

In the world of whole grains, bulgur is analogous to lentils in the legume world. Bulgur is very quick and easy to prepare and goes well with fruits, vegetables, and many fresh herbs. All whole grains have nutrients and dietary fiber, which have come to be associated with lowered risk for heart disease, prevention of colon cancer, and prevention and control of diabetes.

One aspect of the traditional Mediterranean diet that contributes to health is the high consumption of complex carbohydrates. Studies have shown that people in Mediterranean countries traditionally derive 30–60 percent of their daily calories from cereals. By comparison the average in the United States is 19 percent (Spiller, *The Mediterranean Diets,* 5).

In Greek the word for "food" is *sitos,* which specifically means grain or bread (Spiller, *The Mediterranean Diets,* 16). A very popular grain in ancient Greece was barley, a mainstay that grew on the thin limestone soil (Spiller, *The Mediterranean Diets,* 16). In the fifth and fourth centuries B.C.E., during the classical Greek era, barley gruel and barley water were recommended for the sick (Spiller, *The Mediterranean Diets,* 13). Ground barley was often used as flour. In Crete barley remains popular; barley rusks (*dakos*) are widely enjoyed. These croutonlike breads are topped with chopped tomatoes, crumbled feta cheese, and oregano.

During the high-protein-diet craze, pasta got a bad name. But runners always valued the energy it provided. Today we have many types of pasta to choose from right in our local markets. Not only do we have whole-grain pasta, but we also have pasta made from spinach and pasta infused with extra protein and omega-3 fatty acids. Converting to healthier pasta is not that difficult; there are many varieties that boast increased fiber and nutrients without a significant change in the taste or texture.

This is a very good time to consider the choices you make in the supermarket. Avoiding highly processed foods will help you consume more complex carbohydrates. Incorporating more nuts, beans, and other legumes into your diet will be a major step toward following a traditional Greek diet. This

Every Athenian bride was required by a law of Solon (594 B.C.) to take to her wedding a phrygetron, a barley roaster. . . . This was evidently a shallow pan with a handle in the shape of a loop into which the thumb was inserted. . . . It would be hung up with the pots. (Gene A. Spiller, The Mediterranean Diets, 19)

chapter provides many one-dish dinners that are simple yet satisfying when served with a salad. If you create meals using recipes from chapters 2 and 3, you may be surprised to find that you don't miss meat.

FAMILY IN GREECE

The Athens Fulbright office had an excellent public-relations department. Their press release about our arrival led family to us as soon as we settled into our apartment. One evening the doorbell rang. Three black-haired and mustached men announced:

"We are Pastides. Are you Pastides, too?"

"Yes, yes. We are Pastides, won't you come in?" I motioned to the couch for them to sit down, wondering if letting them in was a good idea. Harris was at the gym, and the children were already asleep. I explained that Harris was expected home any minute and got them a cold drink. The three sat on the long couch. Leaning in with the expectation that I would understand them and beginning slowly in their best English, they said:

"Your husband's father. . . ."

"Yes, yes, my father-in-law, go on. . . ."

"Your husband's father . . . had relations . . . with our mother."

"Oooooh, I see." All I could think was, wait until Harris hears this! As soon as he walked in the door, I said:

"Honey, these men are Pastides. . . . Apparently, um, well, your dad had relations with their mother!"

"What?" Harris was smiling at the fellows but looking sideways at me.

"*Nay, nay*" (Yes, yes). Now they were all chattering in Greek one after the other and sometimes two at once. Harris's Greek was good, and he soon realized that what they meant to say was that their mother was related to his father; in fact they were first cousins. The scandal was settled. We learned about their families and the other relatives scattered about Greece and received the first of many family invitations.

In Athens, Harris also had a second cousin, Barbara, from his mother's side of the family. She was a sweet, lighthearted woman who had two children, George and Christina; a wonderful husband, Costas, who was a retired mason; and a sister, Fay, who had Down's syndrome, living with her.

Barbara tracked us down via the same Fulbright press release and immediately invited us for coffee on a Sunday afternoon. I was delighted!

"We'll bring a cake!" I had visions of stopping by one of the many bakeshops I passed on foot as I headed to the market every other day and choosing something pretty that would be packed in a box and tied with a bow. The fruit tarts were always beautiful, glazed berries atop a cushion of custard.

"Okay, honey, we'll see you at three."

Barbara's small apartment was in Kallithea, and we drove around congested streets struggling to read street signs while the locals behind us honked their horns impatiently. Finally on the correct street, we were met by George, who was about fifteen at the time and was standing next to his father's car right outside their building. He waved his arms when he figured out that we were the family he was waiting for. Then he immediately transformed from the welcoming committee to the parking attendant by banging the hood of his father's car, signaling him to move and then motioning for us to park in the newly vacated spot.

We all got out of the car, hugged George, followed him into the building, and crammed into the tiny elevator. No sooner had the elevator door opened than Barbara, Christina, and Fay flowed from the apartment, cooing at the children. We were all embraced and brought into the living room. Fay, who remembered meeting "little Harry" as a child, hugged him tightly and wouldn't let go. Katharine and Andrew were quiet at first, but Christina (thirteen years old) spoke English well and quickly became their playmate.

I handed the cake box to Barbara, who was already asking what we wanted to drink. 'We'll have a drink first and then we'll eat something, okay?" Barbara inquired. "How are you, not too hungry to wait?"

"No, no we're fine." By then Costas had found another parking place and joined us with another round of hugs. Costas spoke no English so he hugged extra hard to make sure we felt welcome.

As it turned out, Barbara and Fay had spent some childhood years in New York and had many fond memories of horsing around at my in-law's apartment. Story after story was told in Greek, English, and "Gringlish"—always with gestures, drama, and comedy. By the end we were all laughing even if we hadn't understood the intricacies of every tale. My children were especially enthralled as Fay told about baby powdering all the coats piled on my in-laws' bed one night when they had a party, which sent Katharine and Andrew into hysterics.

When the laughter died down, Barbara called us to the dining room where we'd expected to have cake and coffee. Instead the long table was completely covered with platters of food. Barbara must have cooked for two days for this presentation.

There were a chicken, a pork loin, and a roasted lamb (even its head was on the platter). There were a huge salad, bread, homemade French fries, hunks of feta, zucchini, stewed greens, and *pastichio.* It was a feast. Costas topped off our juice glasses of retsina wine as needed and carefully selected the tenderest slices of meat for the children. He was the king of this banquet, feeding the masses, observing what each one liked, and passing more of the same. I'm sure he ate, but all I remember is Costas serving us.

For me the most precious moment of communication between Costas and his English-speaking family was his doling out fresh fruits from a bowl broader than his wide chest to each person around the table. He cut and tasted three oranges before hitting one that was good enough for us to share.

In that small apartment above a crowded street, the family sat elbow to elbow around a table that just fit the room. The meal probably represented their food budget for the week. It was at least ten before we hugged good-bye with a background of excited chatter of our next meeting.

The meaning of family in Greece had been defined. The cake stayed in its pretty box and wasn't missed.

Bulgur and Bright Lentils

BOIL THREE CUPS OF WATER in a small saucepan. Rinse the lentils and pour them into the pan of boiling water. Let the lentils boil for only three minutes and then drain them and run cold water over them to stop the cooking. Put the lentils in a small bowl and sprinkle them with 2 tablespoons of fresh lemon juice. Set aside.

Chop the onions and zucchini finely, so the pieces are approximately ¼ inch in size. Heat the olive oil over medium heat in a large sauté pan and slowly sauté the onions and zucchini until soft. Add the minced garlic; stir and cook for a few minutes longer.

When the onions and zucchini are soft, add the cumin, pepper, and raisins; stir to combine. Add a sprinkle of cayenne pepper if you wish— a little goes a long way! Lower the heat and cook for a minute or two, while you boil water for the bulgur. When the water is boiling, stir the bulgur into the sauté pan and blend gently with the vegetable mixture. Pour 2 cups of boiling water into the pan, cover and let simmer for approximately 30 minutes, until the water has been absorbed.

When all the water has been absorbed, combine the lentils with the bulgur mixture, transfer the Bulgur and Bright Lentils to a large serving bowl, and gently stir to combine. Add sea salt to taste and top with fresh, chopped parsley.

This dish is best served at room temperature.

Serves 8–10 as a side dish

1 cup orange (sometimes called "red") split lentils

2 tablespoons fresh lemon juice

1 medium onion, finely chopped

2 cups zucchini squash, finely chopped, about 2 medium squash

2 tablespoons olive oil

2 cloves garlic, minced

1 teaspoon cumin

Black pepper

¼ cup raisins

Sprinkle of cayenne pepper (optional)

1 cup bulgur

2 cups boiling water

Sea salt

Fresh parsley, chopped for garnish

I like to use Heartland Bulgur (see cooking instructions on page 30).

Lentil and Tomato Soup with Coriander and Cumin—*Fakies*

This is a very easy, basic soup. In fact, if all you have in your kitchen is onion, garlic, a can of tomatoes, and lentils, you can make a perfectly fine soup. On their own lentils have a very nice mildly sweet flavor, or you can "doctor them up" with anything you have a taste for, or anything that happens to be left over in your refrigerator. On various occasions I've added yellow squash, zucchini, and sweet potatoes. The more vegetables you add, the more colorful and delicious this soup becomes.

For this lentil soup, I chop the vegetables as small as I can so they conform closely to the size of the lentils. Watch out for your fingers! The seasonings in this recipe are subtle. If you wish, you may intensify them by adding a bit more to suit your taste.

Traditionally in Greek lentil soup, something sour is added just before serving, either lemon juice, yogurt, or vinegar. You can leave the condiments on the table if you wish and allow your guests to choose.

IN A LARGE STOCKPOT, heat the olive oil over medium heat and sauté the finely chopped onions and carrots until the onions are soft. Add the minced garlic and sauté for a few minutes until the garlic begins to brown. Add the tomatoes, coriander, and cumin. Stir and cook for a few minutes to blend the flavors. Add 2 quarts of water. Cover the pot and bring it to a boil, then add the lentils. When the soup returns to a boil, lower the heat and let it simmer, covered. Simmer for about 1½ hours. Add the chopped parsley for the final 15 minutes. Add sea salt and pepper to taste.

Serve hot with a dollop of plain yogurt.

Serves 6–8

2 tablespoons olive oil

2 medium onions, finely chopped

4 large carrots, finely chopped

4 cloves garlic, minced

1 28-ounce can diced or crushed tomatoes (or 3½ cups local tomatoes diced or grated)

1 cup dry whole lentils, rinsed and drained

1 teaspoon ground coriander

1 teaspoon ground cumin

2 quarts water

⅓ cup fresh parsley, chopped

Sea salt
Pepper

Plain yogurt for a condiment

Fruited Chickpeas with Brown Rice

COOK THE BROWN RICE according to package directions. While the rice is cooking, heat the olive oil in a large sauté pan over medium heat and sauté the chopped onions until soft. Add the chopped tomatoes and cook just for a minute or two. Add the chopped dates, ground cumin, and ground cloves and stir all together. Add the strained chickpeas and the white wine. Cook over medium heat, stirring occasionally, until the liquid is reduced by about half. When this sauce is reduced, taste it and add sea salt and pepper according to your taste.

Toast the pine nuts in a dry sauté pan over medium-high heat until they are brown. This will just take two to three minutes. Set them aside.

Cut the tangerine into small pieces. Set aside.

When the brown rice is ready, spoon it onto individual plates. Top the brown rice with a generous serving of the chickpea mixture. Then garnish it with toasted pine nuts and tangerine pieces.

Fruited Chickpeas with Brown Rice is delicious served immediately as described or served after it cools to room temperature with a dollop of plain yogurt.

Serves 4–6 as a main dish

1 cup brown rice

2 tablespoons olive oil

1 medium-size yellow onion, chopped small

3 medium-size ripe tomatoes, chopped small

½ cup pitted dates, chopped

1 teaspoon ground cumin

½ teaspoon ground cloves

1½ cups canned chickpeas, drained

⅓ cup white wine

Sea salt and pepper

For garnish:

⅓ cup toasted pine nuts

1 fresh tangerine, peeled, cut, and seeded

Spinach and Brown Rice—*Spanakorizo*

1 cup brown rice

3 tablespoons olive oil

4 scallions, diced

8 cups fresh spinach leaves, washed, dried, and chopped

1/4 cup chopped fresh dill

Sea salt and pepper

Juice of 1/2 lemon

4 thin lemon slices

COOK THE BROWN RICE according to package directions.

While the rice is cooking, heat the olive oil in a large sauté pan over medium heat and sauté the diced scallions until soft. Add the chopped spinach and cook while tossing until it becomes wilted, just a minute or two. Remove the pan from the heat and set it aside. When the rice is fully cooked, add the rice to the sauté pan. Stir to combine the rice with the sautéed spinach and scallion mixture. Stir in the fresh chopped dill, add sea salt and pepper to taste, and transfer the dish to a serving bowl. Sprinkle with lemon juice and garnish with lemon slices.

Serve immediately or at room temperature.

Serves 6 as a side dish

SPANAKORIZO CHEF'S LUNCH

A tasty "chef's lunch" may be made with your leftover *spanakorizo*. Transfer leftover *spanakorizo* into a small, covered baking dish. Top with crumbled feta cheese, sliced tomato, and dried oregano. Cover and bake at 350 degrees until heated through. This is a delicious take-off on *feta saganaki*.

Pasta with Arugula, Tomatoes, Feta, and Kalamata Olives

The blend of flavors in Pasta with Arugula, Tomatoes, Feta, and Kalamata Olives belies the simplicity of its preparation. As with all Mediterranean recipes, the freshness of the ingredients is the key to the flavor. Freshly picked arugula from the garden is very peppery, and ripe grape tomatoes are sweet. Sheep's milk feta has a much deeper feta taste than cow's milk cheese, and kalamata olives have a rich briny taste. (Goat's milk feta is also available, but I find the flavor too strong and tangy. It stands out in a recipe rather than playing a more cooperative role.) Together the flavors meld as in the classic Greek salad. This is a wonderful recipe for a fast weeknight supper, as the only thing you have to cook is the pasta!

1 pound whole-wheat penne pasta
1 pound sheep's milk feta cheese
2 cups grape tomatoes
3 cups arugula leaves
1$\frac{1}{2}$ cups pitted kalamata olives

This pasta needs no sauce. The flavors of the arugula, tomatoes, feta, and olives are enhanced just from being blended with the hot pasta.

PREPARE THE PASTA according to package directions. While the pasta is cooking, crumble the feta cheese and set it aside. Wash and dry the grape tomatoes and set them aside. Wash and dry the arugula leaves and roughly chop them into 2-inch pieces. Strain any liquid from the kalamata olives and set them aside.

When the pasta is cooked, drain it in a colander and return the pasta to the pan in which you cooked it, now off the heat. Add all the remaining ingredients and toss well. The heat of the pasta and the pan will wilt the arugula a bit and blend the flavors. Transfer the Pasta with Arugula, Tomatoes, Feta, and Kalamata Olives to a serving bowl and serve hot.

Serves 6–8

Acorn-Squash and Ginger Soup with Chickpeas

BOIL THE UNPEELED ACORN SQUASHES and peeled sweet potatoes whole until they are fork tender. Remove them from the water and set aside to cool.

Heat the olive oil in a stockpot over medium heat. Add the julienned ginger and thinly sliced leeks and sauté them until soft. Remove from heat and set aside.

When the squashes have cooled enough to handle them, peel them and discard the peel. Cut each squash in half and discard the seeds and any fibrous parts. Cut the squash and sweet potato into pieces and puree them in a food processor, pulsing until smooth. From the stockpot, add the oil, ginger, and leeks and pulse again until all the contents of the food processor are smooth and well combined.

Pour this puree into the stockpot and add about 2 cups of water. Add the strained chickpeas. Stir to combine and heat the soup to boiling.

When the soup is heated through, assess the consistency. If the soup seems too watery, cook it uncovered for a few more minutes until it thickens. If the soup is too thick, add a bit more water.

Season the soup with sea salt and pepper to your taste. Transfer the Acorn-Squash and Ginger Soup with Chickpeas to serving bowls and garnish with chopped fresh thyme.

Serves 6–8

2 medium acorn squashes
4 large sweet potatoes, peeled
⅓ cup olive oil
3-inch piece fresh ginger, peeled and thinly julienned
2 leeks, sliced into thin slices
2 cups water
1 15-ounce can chickpeas, strained, liquid discarded
Sea salt and pepper
¼ cup chopped fresh thyme for garnish

Cabbage and Apple Bulgur

The inspiration for this dish is derived from traditional Cypriot cracked wheat, usually cooked with chicken stock, onions, and a little vermicelli. Instead of chicken stock, my version is prepared with a "vegetable stock" made from boiling the cabbage and apples.

HEAT THE OLIVE OIL in a large sauté pan over medium heat and sauté the onions, stirring occasionally, until tender and golden.

While the onions are cooking, cook the cabbage in 3 cups of boiling water. When cabbage is tender, add the apples and cook for just 2 minutes.

Reserving the cabbage/apple water, drain the cabbage/apple mixture and set it aside. Return the reserved water to the pan and bring it to a boil.

When the onions are tender and golden, add the minced garlic, the grated ginger, and sea salt and pepper to taste. Cook for a few minutes longer.

Add the bulgur to the sauté pan and pour in 2 cups of the reserved cabbage/apple water. Stir to combine, cover the pan, turn the heat to low, and simmer. Check occasionally and stir to determine whether you need to add more water. Bulgur should be fully cooked at about 30 minutes.

When the bulgur is done, add the cabbage and apples and stir gently to combine. Remove to a serving bowl.

This dish may be served immediately, but is also delicious at room temperature.

Serves 8–10 as a side dish

2 tablespoons olive oil

1 medium onion, finely chopped

3 cups cabbage (approximately ½ an average-size head), chopped small

2 apples, washed, cored, and chopped small (with skin)

2 cloves garlic, minced

2-inch piece of fresh ginger, grated (approximately 2 tablespoons)

Sea salt and pepper

1 cup bulgur

Apple skin is rich in nutrients, and its color adds to the beauty of the dish.

I like to use Heartland Bulgur (see cooking instructions on page 30).

Vegetables Stuffed with Barley—*Gemista*

These days in Greece and Cyprus, vegetarian *gemista* are commonly stuffed with white rice and mint. If you prefer, you may use brown rice.

Barley is a whole grain that the ancient Greeks ground to make bread. The kernels of barley soften when cooked, so the texture is similar to that of rice, though the barley kernels are larger. Barley doesn't impart a strong flavor of its own.

Try this recipe with both brown rice and barley, and then use the grain you prefer—anything goes as long as you're getting a whole grain, fresh veggies, and that healthful olive oil!

2 cups barley

2 colorful peppers

2 onions, peeled

2 tomatoes

½ cup olive oil

3 cloves garlic, minced

½ cup finely chopped
   fresh mint leaves

¼ cup finely chopped
   fresh parsley

Sea salt

Pepper

COOK TWO CUPS OF BARLEY according to the package instructions and set aside.

Wash the peppers, onions, and tomatoes. Cut off the tops and hollow them out. Discard the pepper seeds. Finely chop the insides of the onions and tomatoes and set them aside.

Heat 3 tablespoons of olive oil in a sauté pan over medium heat. Sauté the chopped onion until it begins to soften and then add the chopped tomato and the garlic. Continue cooking until the onion is tender when pierced with a fork. Add the chopped mint leaves, parsley, and sea salt and pepper to taste. Stir the mixture and cook for just a couple of minutes to combine the flavors. Remove the pan from heat and stir the tomato-onion mixture into the cooked barley.

Preheat the oven to 375 degrees.

Brush the bottom of a heavy covered casserole with olive oil. Line up the pepper and onion shells in the pan. Brush each generously with olive oil and sea salt and pepper each shell. Fill the shells with the barley stuffing. Drizzle with the remaining olive oil. Cover the casserole and place it in the middle of the oven. Start the stuffed onions and peppers first as they will need about 40 minutes to cook. While the onions and peppers are cooking, stuff the tomatoes with the remainder of the barley stuffing. After about the first 20 minutes of baking time, add the stuffed tomatoes to the pan, cover again, and bake for 20 minutes more.

Allow the vegetables to cool slightly before serving. *Gemista* is one of those dishes Greeks often eat at room temperature, for as it cools the flavors are enhanced.

Serves 6–8 as a side dish

Gingered Brown Rice
with Raisins and Orange

1 tablespoon olive oil

2 cloves garlic, minced

2 tablespoons grated
  fresh ginger

1 cup brown rice

$\frac{1}{2}$ cup golden raisins

$\frac{1}{4}$ teaspoon sea salt

2 cups boiling water

1 large Minneola orange
  or blood orange

HEAT THE OLIVE OIL in a medium saucepan over medium heat. Sauté the garlic and ginger briefly to flavor the oil, being careful not to burn the garlic.

Add the rice and stir once to combine with the garlic and ginger. Add the boiling water, raisins, and sea salt.

Cover the pan, raise the heat to high, and bring the water to a rolling boil. When it is boiling, reduce the heat to low for 50 minutes to 1 hour or until all the water is absorbed. Transfer the rice to a serving bowl.

Peel and quarter each segment of the orange to create small uniform pieces. Remove the seeds and reserve any juice that escapes.

Add the orange pieces and the juice to the rice and toss. Serve at room temperature.

Gingered Brown Rice with Raisins and Orange is a lovely side dish for any grilled fish, or it is delicious served with hummus and pita bread for a light lunch. It is also good garnished with a dollop of plain yogurt and a sprig of mint leaves.

Serves 6 as a side dish

Carolina Plantation Brown Rice is wonderfully aromatic and easy to cook. If using it, you will need $2\frac{1}{2}$ cups of boiling water for 1 cup of rice, and the cooking time will be only 25–30 minutes.

Sautéed Broccoli Rabe with Penne Pasta

This dish is one of my all-time favorites. It is quick and easy and very healthful. The dark-green leafy vegetable, olive oil, and fresh garlic make a winning combination. The following recipe is a basic version, but it can be easily altered to suit your personal taste. By adding beans, such as white cannellini, or sautéed shrimp, you can create a one-dish meal that is satisfying both for its flavor and for its nutritional value.

Choose any green you like. Broccoli rabe has a bitter flavor, mustard greens are hot, kale is hearty, and spinach is universally enjoyed. All these greens are wonderful prepared according to this recipe. You can also vary this dish by serving it over brown rice instead of pasta, or by using the greens with garlic as a pizza topping.

TRIM AWAY THE THICK STEMS of the broccoli rabe, wash it, and dry it. A salad spinner works well. It's important that the broccoli rabe be dry, or the oil will splatter. Finely chop the broccoli rabe.

In a large sauté pan, heat the olive oil over medium heat and gently sauté the garlic until it is light brown. Add dry, chopped broccoli rabe. Sprinkle with red-pepper flakes and sea salt according to taste. Cook, stirring occasionally, until the greens are wilted, approximately 5 minutes. Remove the pan from the heat.

Boil the pasta according to directions on the package until it is cooked al dente. In other words it should be tender but not mushy.

Strain the pasta and add it to the pan of greens. Place over medium heat and toss to combine. Sprinkle with grated Asiago cheese and serve warm.

Serves 3–4 as a side dish

4 tablespoons olive oil
1 large bunch broccoli rabe
6 cloves garlic, minced
Red-pepper flakes
Sea salt
$\frac{1}{2}$ pound whole-wheat penne pasta
Asiago cheese, grated

Lima Bean and Carrot Soup—*Gigantes*

The name *gigantes* refers to the giant beans used in this soup. Large lima beans work well. *Gigantes* is consumed all over Greece, especially during the Lenten season.

2 cups large dried lima beans

3 quarts unsalted water

4 tablespoons olive oil

2 medium onions, chopped

6 large carrots, peeled and chopped into ¼-inch rounds

6 stalks celery, washed, tops removed, and chopped roughly the same size as the carrots

3 cloves garlic, minced

2½ heaping tablespoons tomato paste

1 quart (4 cups) vegetable stock

Juice of 2 lemons

1 quart boiling water

Sea salt

Pepper

SOAK THE LIMA BEANS for a minimum of 4 hours and rinse. Set aside. Place a large pan of unsalted water (approximately 3 quarts) over high heat and boil. When the water is boiling, add the beans and boil for 20 minutes.

While the beans are boiling, make the soup base in a large stockpot. Start by heating the olive oil over medium heat and adding the onions, carrots, and celery. Cook for 15 minutes, stirring occasionally.

Add the minced garlic and the tomato paste and cook for another 5 minutes. Then add the vegetable stock and lemon juice and raise the heat, bringing the soup to a boil.

In a teapot boil approximately 1 quart of water.

Strain the beans and add them to the stockpot. Pour the boiling water from the teapot until the beans are just covered.

Cover the pot, reduce the heat, and simmer for 2 hours. Remove the lid and simmer uncovered for another 30 minutes.

During the final 30 minutes, some of the water will evaporate and the soup will become thicker. Add sea salt and pepper to taste.

Reheating it before serving will thicken the soup even more. *Gigantes* is delicious when served with extra lemon wedges, black pepper, crusty bread, and salad.

Gigantes freezes well.

Serves 12

Black-Eyed Peas and Swiss Chard—*Lahana me Louvia*

1 bunch Swiss chard

1 cup dried black-eyed peas

3 tablespoons lemon juice

2 tablespoons olive oil

1 small red onion, finely chopped

1 clove garlic, minced

1 teaspoon lemon zest

Sea salt and pepper

WASH AND DRY THE SWISS CHARD, trim away tough stems, and chop the leaves into bite-size pieces.

Rinse the black-eyed peas and set them aside. Boil a quart of water in a medium-size saucepan. Add the black-eyed peas and boil for 2 minutes.

Strain the peas and discard this water, which will be black.

Return the peas to the pan; add enough water to cover the peas by at least 2 inches. Add 1 tablespoon of the lemon juice. Bring to a boil, cover, reduce heat, and simmer for 35–40 minutes until peas are tender. Remove from heat, drain, and set aside.

In a frying pan, heat the olive oil and sauté the chopped onions until soft, then stir in the minced garlic. Stir and cook the onions and garlic for a few minutes until they brown a bit.

Add the Swiss chard and cook for just a few minutes until it is wilted. Add the remaining 2 tablespoons of lemon juice and the lemon zest and stir gently.

Combine onion and Swiss chard mixture with black-eyed peas, and add sea salt and pepper to taste.

This dish may be served warmed or at room temperature. Serve with extra lemon juice or vinegar on the table as condiments.

Serves 6 as a side dish

If you are a garlic lover, an additional clove or two would be great—though the flavor of the black-eyed peas is very good by itself.

Grilled Swordfish with Tomatoes and Sage, p. 125

4. SEAFOOD

■

Seared Shrimp with Red-Pepper Flakes and Basil—*Garides*

Snapper with Lemon and Oregano Sauce—
Snapper with *Ladolemono*

Poached Tilapia with Fennel

Herbed Swordfish Kebabs—*Xifias Souvlaki*

Grilled Tuna with Spicy Peach Chutney

Tomato, Feta, and Shrimp *Saganaki*—*Garides Saganaki*

Grilled Swordfish with Tomatoes and Sage

Salmon Grilled in Grape Leaves

Dorado with Grapefruit and Avocado

DURING THE 1980S AND 1990S, those of us who believed we could be healthier by controlling our diets focused on reducing dietary fat even below the recommended 20–30 percent of our daily intake. Since most Americans consumed a diet far too rich in fats, lowering fat intake was then, and remains today, reasonable advice.

People who were really driven did everything in their power to eliminate all fat from their diets. This intention to lower fat gave rise to a whole line of fat-free foods, which gave consumers a false sense of protection. These new fat-free items were processed foods with artificial fat substitutes and preservatives, and fat was often replaced with increased sugar—not exactly healthier! Even people who avoided these processed foods and tried their best to eat a pure fat-free diet didn't necessarily lower their risks of disease. I remember my dentist, a slim woman with a family history of high cholesterol, relating her disappointment when she had strictly eliminated fat from her diet yet still had a total cholesterol level of over three hundred.

The motivation to lower cholesterol, thereby reducing cardiovascular risk, and to avoid cancers that were thought to be associated with high fat consumption was good, but since then nutritional research has elucidated the role of fats, and dietary advice on fats has changed. The Nurses' Health Study revealed that lowering fat consumption alone did not protect women from heart disease but that changing the type of fat consumed did.

"GOOD OILS": OMEGA-3 FATTY ACIDS

We now know that there are good fats and bad fats. The general rule of thumb is that fats from animal sources are bad while fats from plant sources are good. There are, of course, exceptions. In the case of animal fats, we know that fish oils are actually healthy for humans; they protect against heart disease and are essential for the development and healthy functioning of the brain.

The body requires omega-3 fatty acids, which support healthy cells especially in the eyes and brain. They also provide hormones that are important for the healthy functioning of human blood, blood vessels, and heart. "Dozens of studies have shown that omega-3 fatty acids prevent heart attacks and sudden cardiac deaths by several mechanisms: preventing erratic rhythms, making blood less likely to form clots inside arteries (the ultimate cause of most heart attacks), improving the balance of cholesterol and other fat particles in the bloodstream, and limiting inflammation (which plays a role in the development of atherosclerosis)." Omega-3 fatty acids are also thought to help control lupus, eczema, and rheumatoid arthritis. They may also protect against cancer (Willett, *Eat, Drink, and Be Healthy,* 85, 87).

Other studies reported by Connie Guttersen, author of *The Sonoma Diet,* indicate that omega-3 fatty acids are also associated with the prevention of Alzheimer's disease and depression. Having learned that omega-3 fatty acids are required by the body to make healthy brain cells, we see how it makes intuitive sense that they would also be required to keep our brains functioning in a healthy manner.

In *Eat, Drink, and Be Healthy,* Dr. Walt Willett recommends eating one or more sources of omega-3 fatty acids every day. These include fish, walnuts, canola or soybean oil, ground flaxseeds, and flaxseed oil. The best sources of omega-3 fatty acids are the fattier fishes such as salmon, mackerel, herring, and sardines, keeping in mind that farm-raised fish reflect what they eat.

If you're worried about fish contamination, limit your consumption of the heavy-mercury fishes. Canned tuna is an inexpensive and accessible source of omega-3 fatty acids, but too frequent consumption of it can lead to mercury poisoning. Currently we're hearing reports of contamination in the feed of farm-raised fish. I try whenever possible to purchase wild seafood, and I also follow the reports available through the South Carolina Department of Health and Environmental Control, which indicate fish-consumption hazards in locally caught fish. If you enjoy freshwater fish, seek out your state's guidance on fish consumption.

These concerns are most significant to pregnant and nursing women and young children. Dr. Willett points out that most people who are in the age range to worry about heart disease should know that the health benefits of eating seafood greatly outweigh the possible risk from mercury or PCBs (Willett, *Eat, Drink, and Be Healthy,* 89).

Years ago I heard Dr. William Castelli from the well-known Framingham Heart Study speak at a conference. I remember his saying, "If you can't be a vegetarian, then eat a vegetarian of the sea." I believe that, among other things, he was referring to shrimp. Soon thereafter we started hearing that shrimp contained high levels of cholesterol and for that reason should be avoided.

Shrimp is high in cholesterol, but it is low in overall fat. Research focused on shrimp consumption and human blood cholesterol does not justify eliminating shrimp from one's diet. In one study volunteers ate ten ounces of shrimp per day for three weeks. Although there was an increase in their LDL levels (bad cholesterol) of 7 percent, they experienced a concomitant increase in their HDL levels (good cholesterol) of 12 percent. The shrimp diet also lowered their triglycerides by 13 percent (Simopoulos and Robinson, *The Omega Diet,* 126). It seems that, with its omega-3 fatty acids and other vitamins and minerals, the overall effect of shrimp is a healthy one.

In *Ultraprevention* Drs. Mark Hyman and Mark Liponis explain that our bodies require a balance of omega fats for healthy cells, organs, and tissues. They suggest that most people would benefit from a balance of omega-3 and omega-9 fats. If you are not a fish lover, you can get omega-3 fatty acids from flaxseed (which the Ancient Greeks ground and baked into their bread), walnuts, omega-enriched eggs, organic canola oil, brazil nuts, and sea vegetables (such as nori, kombu, wakame, and dulse). Omega-9 fatty acids are derived from olive oil, avocados, and nuts (Hyman and Liponis, *Ultraprevention,* 127).

I hope the recipes in this chapter will encourage you to try a variety of fish and will provide ways to prepare fish that make it more delicious than ever before.

A FISH TALE: MY FIRST *BARBOUNI*

Harris's host for his Fulbright work in Greece was Dr. Dimitrios Trichopoulos, an internationally renowned cancer epidemiologist.

Soon after we arrived, Dr. Trichopoulos invited us out to dinner with his wife and several senior colleagues from the medical university. We went to an elegant formal restaurant with serious waiters. Dr. Trichopoulos quietly translated the menu and urged me to try the *barbouni,* a small 7–8 inch red mullet. He assured me that *barbouni* was the sweetest and most delicate of the fresh fish. I was easily persuaded, as was the man seated to my right, who was a surgeon.

When our dinners were served, I was a bit taken aback to see the whole mullet on my plate. It had been lightly breaded and pan fried. Its skin was a shiny deep-coral color. It had glassy onyx eyes. I assumed it had been de-boned in the kitchen, but my first bite revealed my mistake. Its delicate flavor was lost in a mouthful of thin bones. Bringing the napkin to my lips, I tried to rid my mouth of bones unobtrusively. I proceeded to pluck tiny pieces of fish carefully from between bones. I wish I could have tasted larger bites of this succulent sweet fish, which was finished with a bright lemon oil and dried oregano.

Meanwhile we shared a lovely bottle of white wine and continuous conversation. Everyone offered advice on how to manage life in Athens, from dealing with public officials whose first answer was always "no" to understanding that people in shouting matches were actually not angry, just exuberant!

One story led to another, but in the midst of collective laughter, Dr. Trichopoulos's face suddenly fell as he looked down at my plate and saw a heap of bones mixed with flesh, head, and eyes still serene. The table drew quiet as our host spoke,

"Patricia, let me order you something else," he pleaded.

"Oh no, I'm just fine," I replied. "It was delicious."

I felt all eyes glance at my neighbor's plate and back at mine. A perfectly intact *barbouni* skeleton sat before him. At my notice the whole table roared. I recovered and defended myself: "No fair, he's a surgeon!"

Seared Shrimp with Red-Pepper Flakes and Basil—*Garides*

Garides is a wonderful buffet dish, which brings rave reviews, and a nice alternative to the standard shrimp cocktail.

1 pound fresh large shrimp

3 tablespoons olive oil

3–4 cloves garlic, minced

$\frac{1}{3}$ cup dry white wine

$\frac{1}{4}$ teaspoon red-pepper flakes

$\frac{1}{4}$ cup finely chopped fresh basil leaves

3–4 whole basil leaves for garnish

Juice and zest of $\frac{1}{2}$ lemon

PEEL AND DEVEIN THE SHRIMP, leaving the tails on. The tails prevent the shrimp from curling during cooking, allowing them to become "finger food" for a buffet. Rinse and then dry the shrimp on towels before cooking.

Heat the olive oil in a large frying pan over high heat, reducing the heat to medium-high if the oil begins to smoke. Place shrimp in one layer in the pan and turn them as soon as the underside looks pink. Cook the second side and remove immediately from the pan. This should take only seconds per side. Continue the process until all the shrimp is cooked. Set cooked shrimp aside.

Lower the heat to medium and add the minced garlic to the pan. Cook for 1–2 minutes, until garlic is golden brown but not burned.

Add the wine to deglaze the pan and turn the heat back up to high. Add the shrimp, red-pepper flakes, and chopped basil and cook until most of the liquid is evaporated (just a minute or two).

Remove the shrimp to a serving dish and sprinkle with lemon juice and zest. Garnish with whole basil leaves.

Serve immediately or at room temperature.

Serves 6 as an appetizer

Snapper with Lemon and Oregano Sauce—Snapper with *Ladolemono*

In Greece lemon and oregano are widely used together as a savory sauce for meats and fish. One of the reasons this combination works well is because Greek lemons are big and juicy and Greek dried oregano is much more fragrant than the typical "spice jar" dried oregano sold in American supermarkets. To enhance the lemon flavor, I add lemon zest with the juice. It really brings out the brightness of the lemon flavor. As for the oregano, many stores in the United States are beginning to carry imported Greek oregano, which is sold in bags containing whole dried stems and leaves. Krinos is one of the exporters; when I find Krinos oregano in the United States, I buy it for my friends and myself. If you can't find it in your local markets, a wonderful substitute is Badia whole oregano, which is sold in the Latino/Hispanic sections of many supermarkets.

PREHEAT THE OVEN to 450 degrees.

Small fish fillets should bake hot and fast so they don't dry out. You can also grill this fish, but use a fish basket as red snapper is fairly fragile.

Wash, pat dry, and set aside the fish fillets.

Zest the lemon, being careful not to include the white pith, which is bitter. Set aside the zest. Juice the lemons.

Put the lemon juice, zest, sea salt, and oregano in a food processor and process slowly while adding the olive oil in a stream. When this sauce is completely blended, pour it into a small pitcher.

Arrange the snapper in a baking dish that just fits it without leaving a lot of extra room. Pour approximately half the sauce over the fish, then rub the fish with the sauce so both sides are coated. Cover the pan and place in preheated oven. Bake for 10 minutes, remove the cover, and bake for 5 minutes more. The fish should readily flake when tested with a fork.

Transfer the snapper to a serving dish with roasted vegetables such as zucchini and potatoes and drizzle the remainder of the lemon-oregano sauce over the fish.

Serves 4

4 6-ounce red-snapper fillets

Zest of 1 large lemon (approximately 2 tablespoons)

Juice of 2 large lemons (approximately $\frac{1}{2}$ cup)

1 teaspoon sea salt

1 teaspoon dried oregano

$\frac{1}{3}$ cup olive oil

Poached Tilapia with Fennel

2 cups julienned fennel

2 tablespoons olive oil

4 small cloves garlic, smashed

½ cup chopped basil leaves

2 tablespoons chopped mint
leaves

2 tablespoons balsamic
vinegar

¼ teaspoon fennel seeds

4 tilapia fillets

¼ cup dry white wine

¼ cup water

Chopped fennel tops for
garnish

TO JULIENNE THE FENNEL, remove the core and slice the bulb into thin, 3-inch-long strips.

Heat the olive oil in a large sauté pan over medium-high heat, add the fennel, cover the pan, and braise it until it begins to soften, shaking the pan occasionally.

Lower the heat to medium, uncover the pan, and add the garlic. Stir and cook for a few minutes, then add the basil and mint, and cook until they are soft and wilted. The fennel should be browned and partially softened.

Add the balsamic vinegar, stirring to deglaze the pan. Stir just until the vinegar is absorbed.

Remove the pan from the heat and stir in the fennel seeds. Set aside.

Light the grill or preheat the oven to 400 degrees.

Set the tilapia fillets on individual sheets of aluminum foil.

Combine the wine and water in a bowl and brush each fillet with this mixture, dampening the fish on both sides. Top each piece of tilapia with one quarter of the fennel mixture.

Fold the foil into a loose packet, enclosing each piece of fish so that moisture will not spill out but leaving some space within for steam to collect. The steam will poach the fish.

Grill for 7–10 minutes or bake for 12–15 minutes until the tilapia is opaque white at its thickest point.

Remove the fish and packet contents to individual plates and top each
with small sprigs of chopped fennel tops for garnish.

Poached Tilapia with Fennel is great with Lemon and Oregano Roasted
Potatoes (page 69) or roasted sweet potatoes and simple grilled vegetables.

Serves 4

Herbed Swordfish Kebabs—
Xifias Souvlaki

PREHEAT THE GRILL to high.

Cut the swordfish steaks into 3-inch cubes and place them in a large shallow bowl to marinate.

In a small bowl, combine the olive oil, oregano, sage, thyme, sea salt, and cracked black pepper. Whisk well. Pour this mixture over the swordfish and let the swordfish marinate for 30 minutes.

Wash the summer squash and zucchini and cut them into 1-inch rounds. Wash the cherry tomatoes. Set aside these vegetables with the pitted kalamata olives.

If you are using wooden skewers, soak them in water first, then put the swordfish, squash, tomatoes, and olives on the skewers, creating colorful patterns. Leave some space between the ingredients so they can cook well.

Grill the *xifias souvlaki* over high heat, turning to cook on all sides, until the swordfish has turned white with golden edges and the vegetables are slightly charred.

Serve with lemon wedges.

Serves 6

2 pounds swordfish steaks
$\frac{1}{2}$ cup olive oil
2 teaspoons dried oregano
1 teaspoon dried sage
1 teaspoon dried thyme
$\frac{1}{2}$ teaspoon sea salt
Several turns of cracked
   black peppercorns
2 yellow summer squash
2 zucchini
1 cup ripe cherry tomatoes
1 cup pitted kalamata olives

1 lemon cut into wedges

Grilled Tuna with Spicy Peach Chutney

Because tuna can dry out easily, it is best served rare. Remember that the tuna will continue to cook a bit after it is removed from the heat source, so don't overcook it. If you *prefer* your tuna well done, Grilled Tuna with Spicy Peach Chutney is a great choice for you because the juice from the peaches adds moisture to the fish.

Peach chutney:

3 large ripe local peaches

5 stalks celery

3 small cloves garlic, minced

1 teaspoon chili powder

Sea salt and pepper, to taste

Grilled tuna steaks:

4 tuna steaks, each about 6
  ounces and approximately
  1½ inches thick

⅓ cup olive oil

Have the tuna steaks cut all the same size and thickness so they will cook uniformly.

BLANCH THE PEACHES in boiling water for just a few (3–4) minutes. Remove them from the water and let them cool.

While the peaches are cooling, wash and finely chop the celery and put it in a medium-size mixing bowl.

When the peaches are cool enough to handle, peel them and cut them into small pieces (about ¼- to ½-inch cubes). Reserve all the peach juices and combine the peaches and the juice with the celery.

Stir in the chili powder and a sprinkle of sea salt and black pepper.

Set the Peach Chutney aside.

Brush the tuna steaks with the olive oil and grill them on a very hot grill for approximately 2–3 minutes per side.

Place the grilled tuna steaks on individual dinner plates and top each with a large spoonful of Peach Chutney.

Serves 4

Tomato, Feta, and Shrimp Saganaki—Garides Saganaki

This recipe is based on *feta saganaki,* but it is zestier because of its added jalapeño peppers. The addition of shrimp makes it a substantial first course or side dish. If it is used as an appetizer, serve it with crusty bread. *Garides saganaki* also makes a great pasta sauce.

2 tablespoons olive oil

2 jalapeño peppers, seeded and finely chopped

1 clove garlic, crushed and chopped

½ pound shrimp, shelled and deveined

½ cup dry white wine

2 teaspoons dried oregano

3 cups ripe, fresh tomatoes, finely chopped or grated (or a 28-ounce can of grated tomatoes, strained of excess juice)

Dash of sugar

8 ounces sheep's milk feta cheese, crumbled

HEAT OLIVE OIL over medium heat in a large saucepan and lightly sauté the chopped jalapeño peppers. Add the chopped garlic and gently sauté for just 1–2 minutes. Add the shrimp and cook just until they turn pink. Add the wine and oregano and stir to combine. Then add the tomatoes and just a dash of sugar. Simmer for about 10–15 minutes, until the tomato juice is reduced by about half. Turn off the heat and add the crumbled feta cheese. It will soften but not completely melt.

Reheat the dish for a minute or so, stirring constantly, before serving.

Serves 4–6 over pasta as a main dish or plain as a side dish

Grilled Swordfish with Tomatoes and Sage

HEAT THE GRILL to high.

Wash and dry the swordfish steaks and brush both sides of each steak with olive oil. Set aside.

Finely chop the jalapeño peppers, discarding the stems, seeds, and ribs.

Heat 3 tablespoons of olive oil in a medium sauté pan over medium-high heat and sauté the jalapeños. When they are beginning to soften, add the cherry tomatoes, cover, and cook for several minutes until they are beginning to burst.

Uncover the pan and cook a bit longer, until the tomatoes are open and cooking down.

Add the chopped sage leaves to the tomatoes and jalapeños and stir to combine. Cook for a few minutes while stirring. Add sea salt and pepper to taste.

Over high heat, grill the swordfish for 3–4 minutes per side.

When the swordfish is cooked, place each piece on a serving tray topped with the tomato, jalapeño, and sage mixture.

4 fresh swordfish steaks
(⅓ pound each, approximately 1-inch thick)
2 tablespoons olive oil
(for coating fish)
2 jalapeño peppers
3 tablespoons olive oil
2 pints ripe cherry tomatoes
¼ cup chopped sage leaves
Sea salt and pepper

Salmon Grilled in Grape Leaves

I first tasted Salmon Grilled in Grape Leaves in a wonderful Middle Eastern restaurant. I was surprised by how appealing the flavor of the grape leaves was when they were charred. I ate the salmon with an American-style Greek salad, and really enjoyed the flavor of the kalamata olives with the salmon. The following recipe joins the marinated salmon with olives, grape leaves, and fresh orange, which I feel brings lightness to this recipe.

32 pitted kalamata olives

½ cup olive oil

4 cloves garlic, minced

Zest of 2 oranges

Juice of 2 oranges

4 skinless salmon fillets,
    4–6 ounces each

16–18 grape leaves (if fresh,
    blanch briefly in boiling
    water)

1 orange for garnish

PREHEAT THE BROILER or grill.

Puree the pitted kalamata olives in the small bowl of a food processor and set aside. In a large mixing bowl, combine the olive oil, garlic, zest and juice of 2 oranges, and pureed olives. Whisk well to combine. Place the salmon fillets in the marinade and let them sit for 15 minutes.

Remove the salmon to a separate bowl. Strain the solids from the marinade, reserving both the solids and the liquid.

Spread two grape leaves out on your work surface so they overlap by about ½ inch where they meet. Place one piece of salmon in the center of the grape leaves and top with ¼ of the solids from the marinade.

Top the salmon with an additional two overlapping grape leaves. Tuck the top leaves under the fish and bring the bottom leaves to the top of the fish so the salmon is completely wrapped in the grape leaves.

Prepare the remaining salmon in the same way.

When all four pieces of fish are wrapped, place them under the broiler or on the grill for 4 minutes, until the grape leaves begin turning black.

Carefully turn each "packet" of salmon and pour the liquid marinade over them. Broil or grill the second side for 4 minutes until the grape leaves are beginning to blacken. Remove the packets to a serving dish.

Cut the orange set aside for garnish in half. Using one half, cut thin slices of orange and place one under each packet of salmon. Squeeze the juice from the remaining orange half over the salmon packets.

Serve immediately.

Serves 4

Dorado with Grapefruit and Avocado

This is a recipe I tasted during a summer vacation in southern France. It's perfect for a hot day as the citrus fruits are so refreshing.

FINELY CHOP half a small onion in a food processor fitted with a steel blade. Add the flesh of four ripe avocados, the juice of two limes, and ½ teaspoon of sea salt and process until you have a smooth puree.

Peel the grapefruits, oranges, and limes with a sharp knife, cutting away all the white pith and squaring off the edges. Cut the fruits into cubes and reserve the juice.

Preheat the grill to high.

On each dinner plate place a heaping serving spoonful of the avocado puree. Place fruit cubes around the plate and pour some citrus juice over them.

Brush the dorado fillets with olive oil and grill them over high heat for approximately 3 minutes per side, or until the fish is opaque and has dark grill marks.

When the fish is cooked, place a fillet atop the avocado puree on each dinner plate. Sprinkle chopped chives over each dish.

Serve immediately.

Serves 4

½ cup finely chopped onion
4 small avocados, peeled and pitted
Juice of two limes
½ teaspoon sea salt
2 pink grapefruits
2 Minneola oranges
2 limes
¼ cup olive oil
4 4-ounce pieces of dorado (mahi-mahi)
½ cup chopped chives

Spiced Lamb Patties—Gyros,
p. 139

5. MEATS IN MODERATION

Chicken Kebabs in Pita Bread—*Kotosouvlaki stin Pita*
Spiced Lamb Patties—*Gyros*
Herb and Garlic Gremolata with Simply Grilled Lamb Chops
Oven-Roasted Stolen Goat—*Kleftiko*
Sage and Thyme Roasted Chicken—*Kotopoulo sto Fournou*
Roasted Lamb with Garlic and Rosemary—*Arnaki sto Fournou*
Yula's Oven-Roasted Onion, Tomato, and Lamb Stew—
Yula's Tavas
Chicken Stew with Artichokes and Lemons—
Kotopoulo Kapama
Herbed Lamb Parcels

SATURATED FAT found in animal products is one of the main reasons to avoid eating meats. Saturated fat is clearly one of the "bad" fats. Red meat has been moved to the top of the food pyramid to indicate that it should be consumed rarely. While we are accustomed to receiving dietary guidance from our cardiologists suggesting we eat less red meat, some research also implicates a diet rich in animal products with common cancers. For example Dr. T. Colin Campbell, author of *The China Study* and himself a vegetarian, considers some well-established risk factors for breast cancer to be early age of menarche, late age of menopause, high levels of female hormones in the blood, and high blood cholesterol. He finds that all are associated with a diet rich in animal products. He summarizes this way: "Women who consume a diet rich in animal-based foods, with a reduced amount of whole, plant-based foods, reach puberty earlier and menopause later, thus extending their reproductive lives. They also have higher levels of female hormones throughout their life span. . . . This idea that breast cancer is centered on estrogen exposure is profound because diet plays a major role in establishing estrogen exposure" (Campbell, *The China Study,* 160).

Books such as *The Omnivore's Dilemma* by Michael Pollan have brought attention to the ways animals are raised in the United States. With our nation's meat industry feeding a corn-based diet laced with hormones and antibiotics to animals on crowded feedlots, many of us are looking elsewhere for pure nutritious foods. Fortunately we have alternative sources of protein that are plant based, and for the special occasions when we would like to eat an animal protein, we have an increasing number of sources for meat from grass-fed, free-range animals.

RANGE-FED ANIMALS

When we consume meat from animals that are allowed to graze, we benefit in two ways. Animals that graze have less saturated fat content in their bodies. In beef, for example, range-fed animals have 500 percent less saturated fat in their tissues than grain-fed beef (Hyman and Liponis, *Ultraprevention,* 126). We also benefit from the omega-3 fatty acids that animals consume when they graze. Range-fed animals eat a much different diet from those of grain-fed animals. Before we started feeding them commercial cornmeal, chickens naturally ate grains, insects, and worms. Laboratory tests showed that the eggs of free-range hens contain twenty times more omega-3 fatty acids than regular supermarket eggs, and this was also true of the animals' flesh (Simopoulos and Robinson, *The Omega Diet,* 29). Not only are free-range animals generally raised without antibiotics or growth hormones, but they are also leaner and provide nutrients that are lacking in grain-fed live-stock.

GOAT MEAT

Goat meat is very popular worldwide and is gaining acceptance in the United States. Also known as "chevron," goat meat offers a high-quality source of protein, a healthier fat content than other cultivated meats, and a good source of iron, potassium, and thiamine. Goat meat has 40 percent less saturated fat than chicken with the skin removed, 800 percent less than beef, 900 percent less than lamb, and 1,100 percent less than pork. With a similar flavor to lamb, chevron is a very healthy and tasty menu choice (Addrizzo, "Use of Goat Milk and Goat Meat").

Many small farms are beginning to raise goats for meat, so if you can't find it in your local market, look online for goat farmers in your area. In the Atlanta area, the DeKalb Farmers Market carries chevron. It may be more readily found in markets that serve an international customer base.

GRILLING WITH OLIVE OIL—A LITTLE COAT OF ARMOR

For decades broiling meat was promoted as the best way to avoid consuming excess saturated animal fat by providing a high heat source and allowing much of the saturated fat to melt and drip away from the meat. But then came the question of possible carcinogens being produced by the grilling process. Research indicated that broiling, deep-frying, and grilling all promote carcinogens in meats because they require very high temperatures.

In traditional Greek grilling, meat is usually marinated first in a mixture that includes olive oil, lemon juice, and oregano. And you can probably guess what research has discovered. Marinating meats in antioxidants such as vinegar, citrus juice, herbs, spices, and olive oil cuts down on the carcinogens. So when grilling, do what Greeks have done for centuries: add this protective coating to your meats.

Enjoy your occasional meat meal and try some of these recipes, which offer small amounts of meat per serving, marinated grilled meats, or very slowly cooked meat, which is soft and satisfying. There's even a goat-meat recipe!

THE EASTER LAMB

In preparation for Easter in Greece, we joined a group of friends from the medical school for a traditional Greek Orthodox Holy Week in the village of Makrinitsa. Makrinitsa is perched on the side of Mount Pelion, just above the city of Volos. Driving up the narrow, winding road to the village, which was founded in the early 1200s, was an experience in nausea control. Round and round, up Mount Pelion we climbed, stopping from time to time for air. As we ascended, a thin veil of mist thickened. We knew eventually we'd be there, and all stomachs would settle, but we had a lingering fear. At the end of Holy Week, we would break our fast and—together with our friends—enjoy a whole baby lamb cooked on a spit, right in front of our children.

Our trepidation stemmed from the reactions Katharine and Andrew had whenever we walked past butcher shops. Whole furry rabbits hung lifeless from hooks in windows and carcasses that looked like small skinned dogs required explanations. Though we looked forward to an authentic Greek Easter, we feared the children's response to taking part in the preparation of the lamb.

The charming village of Makrinitsa was worth the unsettling ride. The monastery that attracted the first settlers was lost to a landslide in the 1600s. But beautiful Old World charm and panoramic views took our collective breath away. Exactly in the town center was a huge living plane tree with a hollowed-out trunk. We stood erect inside this grand tree as its leaves rustled majestically.

We fasted during Lent and ate nothing but beans during the last days of Holy Week; yet we all adored *gigantes* (recipe page 104) with crusty bread. We attended church services in dark caverns of churches where pillars and carvings had withstood centuries. Incense visibly hung in the air, and our children delighted in carrying their very own lighted candles.

The services were dramatic: the smells, the candles, the ancient chanting, the darkened Byzantine icons—it was mystical. We were in church on Holy Thursday night, Good Friday night, and Saturday morning, when we toured five or six local churches to compare their *epitaphios*. An *epitaphio* is a beautifully carved wooden structure bearing an embroidery of the body of Christ. The women in Orthodox churches take great pride in decorating the *epitaphios* with fresh flowers. On Good Friday night, the *epitaphios* are carried through the dark streets, followed by the congregations with their candles. On Saturday morning, when our friends suggested we visit the local churches to view their *epitaphios,* we did so with four small children in tow, and not one complained.

After a spectacular Resurrection service at midnight, which ended with some very modern fireworks, we returned to our inn early Sunday morning and snuggled down to sleep. In the darkness Katharine asked,

"Mom, is there church tomorrow?"

"No dear, we celebrated Easter tonight; there is no church tomorrow."

"Too bad," declared Andrew, heaving a long sigh.

The children fell off to sleep while I worried about the lamb.

I awoke with the sun streaming in the window and two excited children filling me in on the early morning activities:

"Mommy, wake up. The men started the lamb for dinner, and it's your turn to turn the spit!"

"Well all right, I'll be down in a minute." I moved quickly not to miss my turn.

Chicken Kebabs in Pita Bread—
Kotosouvlaki stin Pita

You can make *kotosouvlaki stin pita* with whatever meat you like. This marinade is just as well suited to chunks of pork or lamb as it is to chicken. Of course you don't need to make this into a sandwich in pita bread. Instead you can grill the skewers of marinated meat and serve them with a traditional Greek salad, *tzatziki sauce,* and your choice of crusty bread on the side.

HEAT THE GRILL or broiler to high.

Slice the boneless chicken breasts into 16 long strips approximately 1½-inches wide and set them in a large shallow bowl.

In a smaller mixing bowl, make the marinade by whisking together ¼ cup of olive oil with the lemon juice, oregano, sea salt and pepper. Marinate the chicken pieces for 20–30 minutes.

Thread the chicken strips onto skewers leaving a little space between the pieces. If the pieces are too close together, they won't fully cook. If you are using wooden skewers, run them under water before skewering the chicken. Grill or broil the chicken, turning the skewers at least once until the chicken is fully cooked, approximately 10–12 minutes on the grill or approximately 15 minutes under the broiler. The chicken is done when it is no longer pink in the center. Avoid overcooking, which will make the chicken dry.

While the chicken is cooking, brush the whole-wheat pita breads lightly with the remaining ¼ cup of olive oil, wrap them in foil, and place them in the oven or on the grill to heat them thoroughly. If you are broiling

4 skinless, boneless
chicken breasts

For marinade:

¼ cup olive oil
Juice of ½ lemon
2 teaspoons dried oregano
½ teaspoon sea salt
¼ teaspoon black pepper

For sandwiches:

6–8 whole-wheat pita breads
Another ¼ cup olive oil
to brush the pita breads
1 medium onion, thinly sliced

Tzatziki sauce (page 12)

the chicken in your oven, just place the foil packet of pita breads under the broiler pan of chicken for about 10 minutes. If you are grilling, place the packets right on the grill for a few minutes, then remove them from the direct flame but keep them on the warming area of the grill to stay warm.

Thinly slice the onion and set it aside.

When the chicken is fully cooked, remove it from the heat and set it aside. Cut pieces of aluminum foil large enough to wrap an individual pita. Place one warmed pita bread on each piece of foil. Top it with 2–3 chicken strips, a few slices of raw onion, and a large spoonful of *tzatziki* sauce (recipe on page 12).

Roll the pita bread around its contents wrapping the foil around it so that one end is open and the other end is tightly closed. That way the sauce won't drip on you when you are devouring your *kotosouvlaki stin pita!*

Serves 6–8

Spiced Lamb Patties—Gyros

HEAT THE GRILL to high.

Combine the ground lamb, diced onion, garlic, parsley, egg, and a sprinkle of sea salt and pepper in a large mixing bowl. Use your hands to combine all the ingredients well.

Take a handful of the meat mixture about the size of two eggs, shape it into an oval, and then pat it into a flat, elongated strip (pat as thinly as possible). Place it on a cookie sheet lined with waxed paper. Repeat with the rest of the meat mixture. You should have about twelve strips. The strips will be sticky, so place the sheet of gyro strips into the refrigerator for 15 minutes to chill.

Pick up each gyro strip with a spatula and place on the hot grill. Flip each gyro strip only once, when it is evident that the meat is browning and beginning to firm. *Gyros* are best cooked to well done and should be crispy on the outside.

Brush the pita breads with olive oil and grill lightly. Slice the onion thinly and set aside.

Serve the *gyros* in grilled pita breads with *tzatiki* sauce (recipe on page 12) and thin slices of raw onion.

Serves 12

2 pounds ground lamb
1 medium onion, diced finely
4 cloves garlic, minced
$\frac{1}{2}$ cup finely chopped parsley
1 egg, slightly beaten
Sea salt and pepper

12 whole-wheat pita breads
$\frac{1}{3}$ cup olive oil
1 onion, sliced thinly

Tzatziki sauce (page 12)

Herb and Garlic Gremolata with Simply Grilled Lamb Chops

Herb and Garlic Gremolata is a fresh condiment for grilled lamb and is derived from the Cypriot version of *souvlaki,* which uses a lot of chopped parsley. With eight cloves of garlic, this gremolata is a nice springtime substitute for *tzatziki,* especially for nondairy eaters.

If you have an herb garden, the spring is a wonderful time to experiment with various blends of herbs, as fresh herbs always brighten a recipe, and the addition of garlic and lemon zest make any combination fail-safe!

FINELY CHOP 2 cups of parsley and ½ cup of mint leaves, discarding the mint stems. Mince the garlic. When zesting the lemons, be sure not to include any of the white pith, as it is very bitter. Combine the parsley, mint, garlic, and lemon zest with ¼ cup of olive oil in a bowl and mix well.

Add sea salt and pepper to the gremolata to taste and set it aside.

Separate the chops by cutting between the bones to create eight thin lamb chops. If you prefer a thicker chop, cut between every other bone to make four thicker chops. Brush the lamb chops with ¼ cup of olive oil and sprinkle with sea salt and pepper.

Grill the chops over a high flame to desired doneness. The thin ones will cook very quickly, in just a few minutes, so don't walk away from the grill!

Serve each lamb chop with a large spoonful of gremolata lavished on the meat.

Serves 3–4

2 cups fresh parsley
½ cup fresh mint leaves
8 cloves garlic
Grated zest of 2 lemons
¼ cup olive oil
Sea salt and pepper

1 rack of 8 small lamb chops
¼ cup olive oil

Oven-Roasted Stolen Goat—
Kleftiko

In Greek *kleftiko* means "stolen goat." The story has it that thieves might steal a goat and then cook it in a covered hole in the ground so no smoke would give them away. In Cyprus a rounded outdoor wood-burning oven that looks like a small igloo is often used to make *kleftiko*. A fire is built inside the oven, and when only embers remain, the *kleftiko* is sealed inside and cooked for hours at a very low temperature. When done, the meat is soft and flavored with herbs.

2 pounds goat meat

For marinade:

3 cloves garlic, chopped
2 teaspoons dried oregano
1 teaspoon dried thyme
¼ cup olive oil
Juice of 1 lemon
½ teaspoon sea salt
Several turns of cracked
   black peppercorns

For roasting:

4 potatoes
2 tablespoons olive oil
½ cup dry white wine
Sea salt and pepper to taste

CUT THE GOAT MEAT into large, 4–5-inch chunks. Place the meat in a glass bowl. In a separate, small bowl, combine the chopped garlic, oregano, thyme, ¼ cup of olive oil, lemon juice, ½ teaspoon sea salt, and pepper to create a marinade. Stir the marinade ingredients together well and pour it over the meat. Rub the meat in the marinade to coat all pieces well.

Let the meat marinate for at least one hour. It can marinate overnight if covered and refrigerated. If the meat has been refrigerated, return it to room temperature before roasting.

Preheat the oven to 325 degrees.

Peel and slice 4 potatoes into ⅓-inch slices and set them aside.

Drizzle the bottom of a large sauté pan with 2 tablespoons of olive oil. Place the pan, uncovered, over high heat on the stove top. When the oil is very hot, add the pieces of meat and sear them, turning each piece periodically to brown it on all sides. Remove the pan from the heat and transfer the meat to a plate.

Add ½ cup of dry white wine to deglaze the pan. Stir the wine in the pan to loosen any bits of meat that are stuck to the bottom and reheat it if necessary to do so. When the bottom of the pan has been deglazed, transfer its contents to an oven-proof covered casserole; cast iron works well. Place the potatoes on the bottom of the casserole, then place the meat on top of the potatoes. Add whatever marinade may remain and sprinkle generously with sea salt and pepper.

Cover the casserole and place it in the preheated oven. Roast for approximately 45 minutes. Check once or twice and spoon liquid over the meat and potatoes so they don't dry out. Since goat meat has very little fat, you may need to add moisture. If so, pour a little additional white wine over the meat. When *kleftiko* is ready, the goat meat will be browned through and the potatoes will be fork tender.

Kleftiko may be prepared ahead and reheated quickly in a hot oven just before serving.

Serves 6

Sage and Thyme Roasted Chicken— *Kotopoulo sto Fournou*

1 free-range whole chicken
  (approximately 3 pounds)

¼ cup olive oil

Sea salt and pepper to season
  chicken

½ cup finely chopped fresh
  sage leaves

½ cup finely chopped fresh
  thyme

¼ cup finely chopped fresh
  oregano leaves

¼ cup finely chopped fresh
  parsley

½ cup dry white wine

2 cups parsnips cut into
  1-inch pieces

1 cup carrots cut into 1-inch
  pieces

3 whole sage leaves for
  garnish

3 4-inch sprigs of thyme
  for garnish

PREHEAT THE OVEN to 375 degrees.

Wash the chicken inside and out and pat dry with a clean towel. Place the chicken in a roasting pan large enough to hold it with a few inches of vegetables all around it.

Pour about half the olive oil on the chicken and rub it all over to coat the skin.

Lightly season the chicken with sea salt and pepper inside the cavity and all over the outside.

Combine the finely chopped fresh herbs in a medium-size bowl. Spoon about half the herbs into the chicken cavity. Spread the remainder of the herbs over the outside of the chicken and press them gently onto the oiled skin to make an even coating all over the chicken.

Sprinkle about half the white wine over the chicken and pour the remainder into the pan.

Place the parsnip and carrot pieces in the pan all around the chicken. Pour the remainder of the olive oil over them and stir to coat them with the oil and wine from the bottom of the pan.

Place the roasting pan in the preheated oven and bake for 1–1¼ hours.

The skin of the chicken should be a deep golden brown all over. Juices from the chicken should be clear.

Remove the roasting pan from the oven and let it sit for at least 15 minutes before transferring the chicken to a platter. Spoon the vegetables around the chicken and garnish the chicken with a few whole sage leaves and sprigs of thyme. Sage and Thyme Roasted Chicken makes a beautiful presentation, and its fragrance is herbal and wonderful.

You can make this dish a couple of hours ahead of time and just heat it in a warm oven (250 degrees) for about 20 minutes before serving, which actually enhances the herb flavors.

Serves 6

Roasted Lamb with Garlic and Rosemary— *Arnaki sto Fournou*

Some of the most wonderful lamb roasts we've ever made have been the ones we've stuck in a hot oven to sear, then turned down the oven and ignored them. Bone-in leg of lamb is a most forgiving meat. I start with a "mirepoix" of sorts in the bottom of a roasting pan: carrots, onions, and celery. Then I rub the lamb with olive oil and lots of garlic. The final touch is chopped rosemary leaves sprinkled over the whole works. At 400 degrees the oven sears the meat. Then I lower the heat to 325 degrees for the remaining cooking time. The result is a leg of lamb that is crispy on the outside, but soft and pink on the inside. This roasted lamb is delicate with the scent of rosemary and savory with the sea salt and garlic.

For gravy I like to combine the lamb juices with the vegetables of the "mirepoix" and puree them to make roast veggie gravy. Roasted

Lamb with Garlic and Rosemary has won over even those who have confessed to not liking lamb heretofore.

PREHEAT THE OVEN to 400 degrees.

Wash and dry the lamb and place it in a roasting pan that fits the whole leg, fat side up. Rub the lamb with the olive oil and pour the remaining oil in the bottom of the pan.

Smash the 12 cloves of garlic with the handle of a heavy knife, remove and discard the skins, and roughly chop the garlic to release its flavor. Rub the cloves of garlic over the meat, and place them all over the leg of lamb. Peel the carrots. Cut the carrots and stalks of celery into thirds and place them in the bottom of the roasting pan. Peel and quarter the onion and place it in the pan as well. Sprinkle the sea salt and pepper over the meat and vegetables.

Remove the leaves from the stems of fresh rosemary. Discard the stems and sprinkle the leaves over the lamb and the vegetables in the bottom of the pan.

Place the roasting pan in the center of the preheated oven and roast the lamb at 400 degrees for 15–20 minutes to sear it. Then lower the oven temperature to 325 degrees and proceed to roast the lamb for another 15–20 minutes per pound. This should result in lamb cooked to medium rare–medium (slightly pink in the center). If you are using a convection oven, the roast will cook more quickly, so you may want to check it at 12 minutes per pound.

When the roast is cooked to your liking, remove it from the oven and let it sit for approximately 15 minutes before slicing. Place the roast on a large cutting board "to rest" so you can use the pan juices to make the gravy. Pour the pan juices and the carrots, celery, and onion pieces into a food processor and puree until smooth. Reheat the gravy with ¼ cup of dry white wine before serving.

Place the sliced Roasted Lamb with Garlic and Rosemary on a serving platter and garnish the platter with fresh rosemary.

Serves 12–14

1 bone-in leg of lamb
  (6–7 pounds)
½ cup olive oil
12 cloves garlic
2 large carrots
2 stalks celery
1 large Vidalia onion
Sea salt and pepper to taste
2 6-inch stems of rosemary
¼ cup dry white wine

Yula's Oven-Roasted Onion, Tomato, and Lamb Stew— *Yula's Tavas*

Tavas is a slow-cooked lamb stew. As it cooks for hours, the meat becomes soft and flavors the vegetables, some of which virtually disappear in the cooking. It's delicious. Cousin Yula's rule of thumb is that whatever quantity of lamb you use, you use the same amount of potato and twice as much onion and fresh tomato.

I like to use fresh plum tomatoes, as they are meatier. But when tomatoes are not in season, I use canned plum tomatoes, and they are fine. I discard the liquid from the cans, however, and use only the tomatoes.

It's a good idea to make too much of this stew because it reheats very well. Like most stews, it's just as good, if not better, the next day.

PREHEAT THE OVEN to 375 degrees.

Cut the lamb into large chunks, at least 2-inch cubes or larger. Bone may be left in, but remove any excess fat and discard it. Sprinkle sea salt and pepper on the lamb pieces and place them in a large roasting pan.

Add the quartered potatoes, onions, and tomatoes to the roasting pan and sprinkle with 4 teaspoons of cumin. Pour the olive oil over the meat and vegetables and stir with a large spoon to combine. When all ingredients are combined, give one additional generous sprinkle of sea salt and pepper over the whole pan.

Cover the roasting pan with a lid or foil and bake in a 375-degree oven for a total of three hours. After one hour, uncover the pan, stir the contents, recover, and roast for another hour. At the end of the second hour, remove the foil, turn the lamb brown side down, and bake uncovered for another hour. This will allow the water that has come from the vegetables to braise the ingredients and ultimately reduce to a small amount of flavorful gravy. During the final hour, check and turn the meat periodically as it browns. When the *tavas* is done, all the lamb will be browned and soft, the potatoes tender, and the onions and tomatoes soft and savory.

Serves 6–8

2 pounds lamb (shoulder or leg)

2 pounds medium-size potatoes, peeled and quartered

4 pounds medium-size yellow onions, peeled and quartered

4 pounds plum tomatoes, quartered

4 teaspoons ground cumin

⅓ cup olive oil

Sea salt and pepper

Chicken Stew with Artichokes and Lemons— *Kotopoulo Kapama*

⅓ cup olive oil

1 onion, quartered

½ head garlic, smashed

4 boneless, skinless chicken
  breasts

Paprika to sprinkle

Cayenne pepper to sprinkle

2 cups dry white wine

6 large potatoes, peeled
  and cut into large chunks

1 teaspoon sea salt

2 bay leaves

2 cups water

18 cooked artichoke hearts
  (approximately 2 14-ounce
  cans)

Zest and juice of 2 lemons

¼ cup fresh basil leaves,
  finely chopped

IN A LARGE SAUTÉ PAN heat the olive oil over medium heat. Add the onion pieces and smashed garlic and sauté until they have browned lightly. As they are cooking, turn down the heat if necessary to avoid splattering and burning the garlic.

While the onion and garlic are browning, wash and dry the chicken breasts and cut them into large pieces. Sprinkle the chicken pieces generously with paprika and lightly with cayenne pepper.

Remove the browned onion pieces and garlic from the sauté pan and set them aside.

Turn the heat up to medium-high and brown the chicken pieces, several at one time, on all sides. Remove the browned chicken pieces to a platter. If the oil begins to smoke or splatter, lower the heat a bit.

When all the chicken pieces have been browned, deglaze the empty pan by adding 1 cup of dry white wine. Cook over medium-high heat while stirring until any remnants of onion, garlic, or chicken on the pan have been released.

Place the pieces of potato in the bottom of a large stockpot and top with the chicken pieces, onion, and garlic. Pour the wine from the sauté pan and an additional 1 cup of dry white wine over everything. Add 1 teaspoon of sea salt and 2 bay leaves to the pan. Finally add just enough water to cover the chicken, approximately 2 cups.

Cover the stockpot and cook until it begins to boil; then reduce the heat and simmer partially uncovered (with the pan lid askew) for approximately 30 minutes until the potatoes are tender and the chicken is fully cooked throughout.

Just before serving, add the artichoke hearts and the juice of two lemons and cook over medium heat until the stew is piping hot and the liquid is reduced by about half.

Transfer the *kotopoulo kapama* to a serving bowl and sprinkle with the zest of two lemons. Garnish with chopped fresh basil leaves.

Serves 6

Herbed Lamb Parcels

These pretty little parcels are full of flavor, blending herbed lamb, tangy grape leaves, and flaky filo. *Tzatziki* sauce (recipe on page 12) is fabulous with any lamb dish, and it works very well with this one.

This is a good example of a flavorful dish that uses only a small amount of meat per serving. I like to pair it with Stuffed Eggplant and Zucchini—*Papoutsakia* (page 72) and an interesting salad, such as Roasted-Beet and Arugula Salad (page 44). A meal like this provides lots of different tastes, many vegetables, and plenty of color on the plate!

For marinade:

¼ cup olive oil

Juice of one fresh lemon

2 cloves garlic, minced

¼ cup finely chopped fresh mint leaves

¼ cup finely chopped fresh oregano leaves

Sea salt and pepper to taste

COMBINE THE OLIVE OIL, lemon juice, garlic, mint, oregano, sea salt, and pepper. Marinate the sliced lamb in this mixture for at least 2 hours. You can leave it overnight in the refrigerator if you wish, but bring it to room temperature before making the parcels, as the olive oil will solidify in the cold refrigerator.

Preheat the oven to 375 degrees.

Unroll the thawed filo with the shorter side toward you on a wax-paper-covered counter. If the filo is sold in two individually wrapped rolls, put the second one back in the refrigerator while you work with the first. Set up next to the stove top so you are close to the melted butter. Melt the salted and unsalted butters together in one small pan.

Brush the top sheet of filo with butter. Place a grape leaf at the end closest to you, with its veins up. Top the grape leaf with a few slices of lamb. Don't stack the lamb; spread it out on top of the grape leaf.

From the lower left-hand corner of the stack of filo sheets, pick up 2 sheets of filo; carefully fold them in toward the center, approximately 1 inch. Butter to secure, and repeat on the right-hand side. Next fold

1 inch of the filo at the end closest to you toward the middle and butter. Then, from the end closest to you, lift the filo, with grape leaf and lamb and fold it away from you to create a parcel about 3 inches wide. Fold the filo from the sides in toward the middle, making the packet about 5–6 inches long, and butter the folds. Fold the packet away from you until you come to the end of the filo sheet, and butter all around this parcel, especially the final fold. Place it on the cookie sheet.

Continue making parcels until all the lamb is used. This recipe makes approximately 20 pieces. Bake the Herbed Lamb Parcels in a preheated 375-degree oven for 25–30 minutes or until they turn a deep golden brown.

If you wish to freeze some lamb parcels, place them uncooked in a rectangular, airtight freezer container. If you have more than one layer of Herbed Lamb Parcels to freeze, place a sheet of waxed paper between each layer. When putting the cover on the container, get as much of the air out of the container as possible. Store the container in the freezer.

To bake frozen Herbed Lamb Parcels, thaw them in the refrigerator for 8–10 hours before baking. Bake as directed above in a 375-degree oven. Baking time may be longer if the parcels are still slightly frozen when you put them in the oven. Do not thaw the parcels on the countertop because the filo will become wet and gummy, which will adversely affect the appearance and taste of these precious parcels!

To reheat previously baked parcels, use a conventional oven. Microwaves make filo dough limp rather than crispy.

Serves 10 for dinner, 20 for appetizers

For parcels:

2 pounds lean lamb, thinly sliced ($\frac{1}{4}$–$\frac{1}{3}$ inch), with fat trimmed and discarded

1 pound prepared, frozen filo, thawed in refrigerator for 24 hours before using

3 ounces unsalted butter, melted

3 ounces salted butter, melted

20 large brine-cured grape leaves

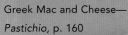

Greek Mac and Cheese—
Pastichio, p. 160

6. SPECIAL-OCCASION GREEK TRADITIONS

■

Traditional *Moussaka*
Greek Mac and Cheese—*Pastichio*

THERE ARE TWO Greek "comfort" foods that are rich and scrumptious and assure wonderful dinner parties. Calling them "comfort foods" is a nice way of saying they have more saturated fat than many recipes in *Greek Revival: Cooking for Life.* Both recipes are made with a béchamel sauce enriched with eggs and cheese. The good news is that by substituting a lean cut of meat and low-fat milk, one can decrease the saturated-fat content, without adversely affecting the flavor at all. In my version of *moussaka,* one broils slices of eggplant and potatoes rather than frying them, which also makes the dish a bit lighter.

If you prefer, it is easy to adjust both of these recipes to make them meatless. I've often made the meat sauce in both recipes without the meat, and have enjoyed *pastichio* with spinach added to it.

Pastichio and *moussaka* are truly crowd pleasers. Make one of these recipes for company, and they will surely be impressed. Shared with friends, *pastichio* and *moussaka* are great "entrées" into the Greek lifestyle; taste, savor, and enjoy.

Traditional *Moussaka*

Moussaka is one of the most flavorful of the traditional Greek *taverna* dishes. The depth and richness of the meat sauce with red wine and a hint of cinnamon, the rich béchamel sauce sharpened with tangy cheeses, and the eggplant and potatoes all come together in this savory *moussaka,* which is perfect when served with a simple salad and crusty bread.

Notice that I do not recommend peeling the eggplant. This is because so much of the flavor is lost without the skin. The skin can be tough, but if you slice the eggplant thinly enough and pierce any large strips of skin, you will successfully cook the toughness out without sacrificing the taste.

Preparing the eggplant and potatoes:

2½ pounds medium egg-
    plants
Sea salt
3–4 large potatoes, peeled

Preparing the meat sauce:

2 tablespoons olive oil
1 medium onion, finely
    chopped or grated in
    a food processor
1 clove garlic, minced
I pound lean ground beef
1 can crushed tomatoes
    (approximately 15 ounces)
3 tablespoons tomato paste
¼ cup dry red wine
1 teaspoon ground cinnamon
½ cup fresh parsley, chopped
Sea salt and pepper
½ cup dry bread crumbs
½ cup grated *kefalotiri*
    cheese (Parmesan, Asiago,
    or Romano may be substi-
    tuted)

Broiling the eggplant and potatoes:

Eggplant slices
Sliced potatoes
½ cup olive oil

WASH AND TRIM the eggplants. Slice them lengthwise into ¼-inch-thick slices. Place the slices in a large colander, salt each layer with sea salt, and place a heavy plate on top. Let the eggplant slices sit this way until you have prepared the meat sauce. This process will draw out the bitterness and much of the natural moisture from the eggplant.

Peel and wash the potatoes and set them aside.

Heat 2 tablespoons of olive oil in a large sauté pan over medium heat and sauté the finely chopped onions. When the onions are golden in color, add the clove of minced garlic, toss to combine, and cook for a few minutes. Add the lean ground beef. Use a spatula to break it apart and brown the meat thoroughly. To this mixture add the canned toma-toes with their juice, tomato paste, red wine, cinnamon, parsley, and a little sea salt and pepper. Stir to combine all these ingredients, then lower the heat and simmer until most of the liquid is absorbed. Remove the pan from the heat and let the sauce cool slightly. Add ½ cup bread crumbs and ½ cup grated cheese. Stir all together and set aside.

Dry the eggplant slices with kitchen towels, then brush them with olive oil on both sides and broil them until they brown. Continue broiling until all the eggplant is cooked. It will only enhance the flavor if some of the skin blackens a bit, but watch carefully so as not to burn the egg-plant.

While you are broiling the eggplant, slice the potatoes lengthwise into ¼-inch slices. Brush these with olive oil and broil them until they are lightly browned.

Preheat the oven to 350 degrees, conventional bake mode.

When all eggplant and potato slices have been broiled, prepare the baking dish. Brush the bottom of an 11 x 13-inch pan with 2 tablespoons of olive oil and sprinkle it with ½ cup bread crumbs. Place the potatoes on the bottom of the pan, followed by a layer of eggplant slices. Then spoon half the meat sauce into the baking dish and spread it over the eggplant. Add the remaining eggplant slices followed by the remaining meat mix-ture. Now you are ready to prepare the béchamel sauce.

Melt the butter in a large saucepan over moderate heat. Add the flour and stir continuously with a wooden spoon until it gets bubbly.

Continue stirring while you add the milk gradually. When all the milk has been added, cook until the sauce thickens and coats the back of the spoon (about 5–7 minutes). Test it by coating the spoon and drawing a line in the sauce with your finger. If the line stays clear, the sauce is thick enough. Remove the pan from the heat, stir in 1 cup of grated cheese, and cool slightly.

Now you are going to add in the eggs. In order for them not to scramble, you should stir some béchamel sauce into the beaten eggs by the spoonful, stirring after each spoonful to raise the temperature of the eggs. After you've added 4–5 spoonfuls of béchamel sauce to the eggs, you can safely add them to the pot of béchamel sauce. Stir the sauce until it is smooth and the eggs are completely incorporated. Add a sprinkle of sea salt and pepper.

Pour the béchamel sauce over the meat sauce in the casserole. Sprinkle the remaining ¼ cup cheese over the *moussaka* and grate the nutmeg generously on top.

BAKING THE CASSEROLE:

Bake the *moussaka* at 350 degrees for approximately 1 hour, until the top is well browned. Do not use convection mode as it is too drying for the béchamel sauce.

Cool for 15 minutes before cutting.

You can prepare *moussaka* a day in advance, refrigerate it, and reheat it just before serving. Take it from the refrigerator a few hours before heating, cut it into pieces while it is still cold, and then reheat it thoroughly. Cover while reheating to avoid drying out the béchamel sauce.

Serves 12

Preparing the baking dish:

2 tablespoons olive oil
⅓ cup bread crumbs

Béchamel sauce:

½ cup butter
½ cup plus 1 tablespoon flour
4 cups milk (1 percent works fine)
1¼ cups grated *kefalotiri* cheese (Parmesan, Asiago, or Romano may be substituted)
3 eggs, brought to room temperature and slightly beaten
Sea salt and pepper
Nutmeg

Greek Mac and Cheese—
Pastichio

Pastichio is a creamy rich version of macaroni and cheese. The original recipe was imparted to me during the cooking lessons I took in Athens. I have "lightened" it slightly by substituting low-fat milk for whole milk and by using the leanest ground meat available. I make it once or twice a year as a "special-occasion Greek tradition," especially for a large crowd so there's not a lot left over to tempt us! Enjoy!

Preparing the meat sauce:

¼ cup olive oil

1 large onion, chopped

1 pound ground sirloin

4–5 fresh tomatoes, grated
    (if not in season, use
    crushed, canned tomatoes,
    28 ounces)

3 tablespoons tomato paste

¼ cup fresh parsley, chopped

1 teaspoon ground cinnamon

1 scant teaspoon sugar

½ cup red wine

½ cup dry bread crumbs

HEAT ¼ CUP OLIVE OIL in a large sauté pan and sauté the chopped onion until it begins to brown. Add the ground meat and cook thoroughly. Stir in the tomatoes, tomato paste, fresh parsley, cinnamon, sugar, and red wine and cook until the liquid is almost completely absorbed. Let this meat sauce cool slightly and then stir in ½ cup bread crumbs.

Boil the macaroni in salted water until tender, but do not overcook the pasta.

Drain the macaroni in a colander. Using the same pan in which you cooked the macaroni, melt ½ cup butter. With the heat turned off, put the macaroni back into the pan and mix it well with the butter. Add 1 cup grated cheese, slightly beaten egg whites, and evaporated milk, stirring after each ingredient to combine thoroughly.

Spray the bottom of an 11 x 13-inch baking pan with olive-oil spray and sprinkle with ¼ cup bread crumbs.

Spread half the macaroni mixture in the pan. Then spread the meat sauce over the macaroni. Finally, spread the remainder of the macaroni on top of the meat sauce. Set aside.

Preheat the oven to 375 degrees, conventional bake mode.

BÉCHAMEL SAUCE:

Melt ½ cup butter in a large heavy saucepan over moderate heat. With a wooden spoon, stir in the flour and cook for 2–3 minutes until it becomes foamy. Add the milk gradually, stirring continuously, and cook until the sauce is thick enough to coat the back of the wooden spoon (about 5–7 minutes). Test it by coating the spoon and drawing a line through the sauce with your finger. If the line stays clear, the sauce is thick enough.

Remove the pan from the heat and stir in ¾ cup grated cheese.

TEMPERING THE EGGS:

Add tablespoonfuls of the béchamel sauce one at a time to the slightly beaten egg yolks, stirring well after each addition to temper the eggs. This process will bring up the temperature of the eggs so they won't scramble when they hit the warm sauce. After 5–6 spoonfuls, you should be able to combine the yolks with the rest of the sauce without scrambling them. Stir the yolks into the sauce to blend. Then add a sprinkle of sea salt and pepper.

Pour the sauce over the macaroni to completely cover the top of the casserole. Sprinkle with nutmeg and then with the remaining ½ cup grated cheese.

BAKING THE CASSEROLE:

Bake the *pastichio* in a 375-degree oven for approximately 40 minutes, until the top is a nice medium brown. Cool for 15 minutes before cutting. Do not use convection mode for baking *pastichio* as it will dry out the béchamel sauce.

Serves 12

Preparing the macaroni:

1 pound macaroni (penne or ziti)
Sea salt for macaroni water
½ cup butter, melted
1 cup grated hard cheese such as *kefalotiri*, Parmesan, Romano, or Asiago)
4 egg whites, slightly beaten (reserve yolks for the béchamel sauce)
½ cup evaporated milk

Preparing the baking dish:

Olive-oil spray
¼ cup bread crumbs

Béchamel sauce:

½ cup butter
½ cup flour
4 cups milk (1 percent works fine)
1 cup grated *kefalotiri* cheese (Parmesan, Asiago, or Romano may be substituted)
4 eggs yolks, brought to room temperature and slightly beaten
Sea salt and pepper
Nutmeg

Chef's Lunch: Arugula, Avocado,
and Basil Salad, p. 169

7. NUTRITION ON THE RUN

■

young woman with short dark hair, glistening eyes, and a bright smile. She loved the apartment but wasn't quite ready to move in. She had some traveling ahead of her before settling down there.

Just a few blocks up the street, in the last building before Total Fitness Gym, lived Angela's English/Irish maternal grandmother Mary. It was agreed that we would pay her the rent, as Nick and his wife lived about an hour away.

Mary was in her early eighties and widowed. Extremely warm and talkative, she had lots of friends and was forever eating out. If you wanted a restaurant review she was ready to provide one. We had no language barrier or shortage of words. One day she offered me a tour of her place, and I noticed immediately a framed picture of George Clooney among her many family photos.

"Mary, are you related to George Clooney?"

"Oh no dear, I just think he's cute."

Then we proceeded down the hall so she could show me her rose bedroom, and pinned to the bathroom door was a handsome 8 × 10 of George clipped from a magazine!

From Angela's apartment, Harris and I walked three blocks to Mackenzie Beach every morning at 6:00 A.M. We would stroll for a few minutes along the surf and swim for twenty or thirty minutes. There was a regular group of morning swimmers, mostly retired men and middle-aged women in groups—bathing-capped friends chatting the whole while. Everyone greeted us, and before long we were compatriots. What an excellent way to start the day! Then we'd go back to the apartment. He'd get ready for work, and I'd dress for the gym.

I arrived at Total Fitness by 8:00 A.M. Monday through Friday. I took yoga classes on Monday and Wednesday, Pilates on Tuesday and Thursday, and dance class on Friday. I was the worst at dance. I always took the back row, where I stayed two or three steps behind the talented dancers. But I did have enthusiasm! After class I'd work out in the gym with super-fit athletic trainers and occasionally stay to swim laps. I'd usually be home by 11:00 A.M. completely famished! So I'd have my yogurt parfait (p. 198), take a nice bath, and start my cooking.

I tested many recipes, all created in Angela's bright and shiny new kitchen. Every pot and pan was christened, as was every appliance, every plate.

Harris was very happy to return home to new meals! We typically enjoyed three dishes each evening, but never before having our evening walk on the beach, and on the warmer days, another swim.

I was hungry, I pulled it out and munched on it plain. It was sweet and delicious. When you begin to eat fruits and vegetables fresh from the garden, just as nature produces them, the flavors become new and wonderful. I enjoy eating fresh produce that we grow ourselves. We use our kitchen compost for fertilizer, no chemical pesticides, and the rainwater collected in our barrels for irrigation. The food is wonderful, and it's so satisfying to be out of a car and close to the earth.

"MIGHTY APHRODITE" CHRISTENS ANGELA'S KITCHEN

We lived in Cyprus during the summer of 2006. Harris worked in the capital of Nicosia on a cancer-registry project there. Cyprus was the homeland of his parents and sister. His family moved to New York in 1947, and he came along in 1954, the first born in America.

We were thrilled as we planned the leave, not simply because it was nice to have a change of venue for three months, but also because we both felt that Harris had the opportunity to "give back" to Cyprus from the fruits of his parents' labors in the United States. He was the first in his family to go to college and then went on to become a Ph.D. epidemiologist and professor. Had his parents stayed in Cyprus, chances are he would not have received a college education because at that time Cyprus had no university, and only children of the wealthy were sent to England to be educated.

While Harris worked on the cancer-registry project, my plan was to test recipes for this book. We contacted some cousins, and they agreed to find us an apartment so we could hit the ground running.

When we arrived we were greeted with loving arms as the long-lost relatives, which was truly humbling and wonderful. On the other hand, the apartment was dismal. Formerly a summer rental on the sea, the neglected apartment had stained carpeting and minimal furnishings, and it was dark, damp, and depressing. The tiny two-burner stove top, dorm-size refrigerator, and limited cookware and utensils were not the set-up I'd imagined.

So on our first free weekend, we set out to find a better living arrangement. We consulted the newspaper and lined up a few visits. By the third stop, we had found it: a newly renovated two-bedroom apartment with a small veranda overlooking the salt lake and beautiful sunsets of Larnaca. It had a brand-new, well-equipped kitchen with great appliances, cookware, and utensils—everything I needed to get started cooking. It was a few minutes' walk to the beach and the gym, and best of all it had no carpeting!

Our new landlord, Nick, had just bought and renovated the apartment for his daughter Angela, who was in her early twenties. Angela was a lovely young woman with short dark hair, glistening eyes, and a bright smile. She loved the apartment but wasn't quite ready to move in. She had some traveling ahead of her before settling down there.

Just a few blocks up the street, in the last building before Total Fitness Gym, lived Angela's English/Irish maternal grandmother Mary. It was agreed that we would pay her the rent, as Nick and his wife lived about an hour away.

Mary was in her early eighties and widowed. Extremely warm and talkative, she had lots of friends and was forever eating out. If you wanted a restaurant review she was ready to provide one. We had no language barrier or shortage of words. One day she offered me a tour of her place, and I noticed immediately a framed picture of George Clooney among her many family photos.

"Mary, are you related to George Clooney?"

"Oh no dear, I just think he's cute."

Then we proceeded down the hall so she could show me her rose bedroom, and pinned to the bathroom door was a handsome 8 × 10 of George clipped from a magazine!

From Angela's apartment, Harris and I walked three blocks to Mackenzie Beach every morning at 6:00 A.M. We would stroll for a few minutes along the surf and swim for twenty or thirty minutes. There was a regular group of morning swimmers, mostly retired men and middle-aged women in groups—bathing-capped friends chatting the whole while. Everyone greeted us, and before long we were compatriots. What an excellent way to start the day! Then we'd go back to the apartment. He'd get ready for work, and I'd dress for the gym.

I arrived at Total Fitness by 8:00 A.M. Monday through Friday. I took yoga classes on Monday and Wednesday, Pilates on Tuesday and Thursday, and dance class on Friday. I was the worst at dance. I always took the back row, where I stayed two or three steps behind the talented dancers. But I did have enthusiasm! After class I'd work out in the gym with super-fit athletic trainers and occasionally stay to swim laps. I'd usually be home by 11:00 A.M. completely famished! So I'd have my yogurt parfait (p. 198), take a nice bath, and start my cooking.

I tested many recipes, all created in Angela's bright and shiny new kitchen. Every pot and pan was christened, as was every appliance, every plate.

Harris was very happy to return home to new meals! We typically enjoyed three dishes each evening, but never before having our evening walk on the beach, and on the warmer days, another swim.

7. NUTRITION ON THE RUN

◼

Chef's Lunch: *Haloumi* and Basil Sandwich

Chef's Lunch: Arugula, Avocado, and Basil Salad

Chef's Lunch: Grilled Gruyère and Arugula Sandwich

ONE OF OUR MOST VALUABLE LESSONS during our two sabbaticals was learned by example from our host cultures. Just as important as food preparation was taking the time to eat, sitting comfortably and enjoying the food in the good company of family and friends. The lesson was, don't eat on the run.

When Andrew returned to fifth grade in the United States after spending the first semester in Geneva, Switzerland, I asked him what was the most difficult aspect of his transition. He didn't hesitate: "lunch."

In Geneva his public school had a two-hour lunch break, during which he walked home to eat with his sister and me at our dining-room table. It was a relaxed lunch period that left time for a game of soccer with friends, review of a French lesson, or just a rest. In his American public school, lunch period was thirty minutes, which included time to wait in the lunch line *and* have recess, so eating was given short shrift. Each table was dismissed for recess when all its children were done eating, so the kids "encouraged" each other with "hurry up!" so they could get outside sooner.

ON FEELING SATISFIED

I'm convinced that one of the reasons we have so many overweight Americans is that we continually eat on the run. From coffee in the car to fast-food drive-throughs, we're trying to squeeze in a meal between children's games, meetings, and multitasking. The average American today doesn't put in much table time. I think we're paying a price for this bad eating behavior. In addition to consuming highly processed, calorie-, sodium-, and fat-dense foods, we also don't take the time necessary to appreciate the sensual satisfaction of our meals, and—after an hour or so—we're looking for a snack. All this running isn't helping to promote a healthy relationship between Americans and food.

When you really need a snack on the run, choose one that nature has provided, full of phytonutrients and ready to eat. A handful of nuts provides protein and fiber, and it's satisfying because it contains a healthy fat. A piece of fruit, such as an apple, just needs a good washing, and it's ready to go anywhere you go. Apples are rich in phenols that prevent free radicals from oxidizing and causing havoc in your body. These phenols have been shown in some studies to decrease heart disease. In addition apples have insoluble and soluble fiber, promoting good digestion and helping to lower cholesterol (Yeager, *The Doctors Book of Food Remedies,* 29–32).

Vegetables can also make wonderful snacks. We had so much cabbage in the garden this spring that I chopped it and kept it in the refrigerator. When

After about a month of this intense exercise routine, Harris claimed I looked better than when he met me at twenty-two. He nicknamed me "Mighty Aphrodite." Sounded good to me—Aphrodite, the goddess of love and beauty, born of sea foam off the coast of Cyprus. Even the ancients felt she was both Greek and foreign. (There's no mention of her dancing aptitude, so I accepted the compliment even though it was untrue!)

So here are a few choice recipes that were by-products of my recipe testing in Cyprus. Made from whatever was left in the refrigerator, they are easy and tasty. These are the "at home" version of fast food, you'll have to stop whatever you're doing for only a few minutes to prepare them. But do sit down to eat. . . .

Chef's Lunch: *Haloumi* and Basil Sandwich

When I was testing recipes in Cyprus, I would make this lunch whenever I had leftover *haloumi* cheese. *Haloumi* is a dense sheep's milk cheese that, when fried, turns crispy and brown, without melting. Many fine cheese shops in the United States now carry *haloumi,* and in Columbia, South Carolina, it is readily available at the Fresh Market.

1 slice of crusty whole-grain baguette, toasted
1 teaspoon olive oil
2 slices *haloumi*, ⅓-inch thick
6 basil leaves
½ fresh lemon

Haloumi *and Basil Sandwich is delicious served with Coriander and Garlic Olives (page 32) or chilled watermelon on a hot day.*

HEAT THE OLIVE OIL in a small frying pan over medium heat. Fry the *haloumi* slowly, turning once until it is crispy and brown on both sides. Arrange the slices on the toasted bread. Using the same pan, fry the basil leaves, turning each one once. They will wilt slightly. Top the *haloumi* with basil leaves and squeeze fresh lemon juice on top. Lunch is served!

Serves 1

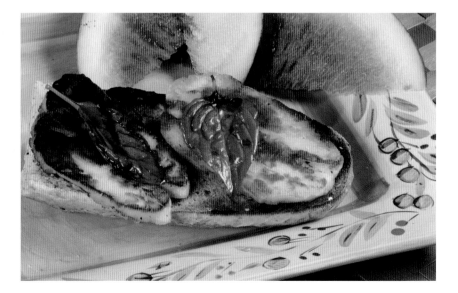

Chef's Lunch: Arugula, Avocado, and Basil Salad

I first made this salad while in the midst of testing recipes. I'd been cooking all morning and was suddenly starved. The ingredients in this salad are some of my favorites. Cooking the basil enhances its flavor, and warming the tomato wedges brings out their flavor and juice, so you can avoid using a heavy salad dressing. It turned out to be a lovely summertime lunch.

PLACE THE ARUGULA in an individual salad bowl and add the avocado slices.

Heat the olive oil in a medium-size sauté pan over medium-high heat. Place the basil leaves in the pan and cook them for 2–3 minutes, turning once. Add the tomato wedges and toss in the pan for 30 seconds. Remove the pan from heat and add the balsamic vinegar to it. Pour the contents of the pan into the salad, toss, and add sea salt and pepper to taste.

Serves 1

1 cup washed and trimmed
   arugula
½ small avocado,
   pitted and sliced
1 teaspoon olive oil
8 small basil leaves, washed
   and dried
1 small tomato cut into
   wedges
1 teaspoon balsamic vinegar
Sea salt and pepper

Chef's Lunch: Grilled Gruyère and Arugula Sandwich

Lunches like this one are so quick, yet so flavorful! It's like a fondue for one or a new take on a *croque monsieur*. Search for an unusual bread that appeals to you. In a sandwich the quality of the bread is critical. I used sunflower- and sesame-seed bread in Cyprus, which was delicious. At the University of South Carolina farmers' market, we have a bread baker who makes 100 percent rye bread, which is rich, dense, and delicious.

If you can afford a nap after lunch, you might find a small glass of dry white wine is the perfect accompaniment to this simple but elegant sandwich!

HEAT THE OLIVE OIL in a small sauté pan over medium heat. Make a sandwich with the bread, mustard, cheese, and arugula. Toast it in the warm pan until the cheese is melted, turning once. A heavy plate placed on the sandwich speeds the melting. (Or if you have a sandwich press, this is a perfect sandwich for it.)

Grilled Gruyère and Arugula is also delicious with a slice of tomato.

Serves 1

1 teaspoon olive oil

2 thin slices whole-grain bread

Spicy Dijon mustard

1 slice Gruyère cheese

4 large arugula leaves

Walnut and Filo Pastry—
Baklava, p. 180

8. NUTS AND SPICES

Healthy Desserts

◾

Anise and Sesame Cookies—*Koulourakia*
Walnut and Filo Pastry—*Baklava*
Cinnamon Cookies with Syrup and Walnuts—*Finikia*
Spiced Berry Soup
Honey Frozen Yogurt
Rose-Scented Custard Pie—*Galaktoboureko*
Greek Wedding Cookies with Almonds—*Kourabiedes*
Rice Pudding with Raisins and Cinnamon—*Rizogalo*
Greek Apple Tart with Walnut-Crumb Topping—*Milopita*
Spiced Walnut Cake—*Karidopita*
Pistachio and Honey Coffee Cake
Yogurt Parfaits with Blueberries and Lemon Curd
Tangiest Lemony Lemon Curd

"EPIDEMIOLOGICAL STUDIES have been remarkably consistent in showing an association between nut consumption and a reduced risk for coronary heart disease," reported Joan Sabaté in an article published in the *American Journal of Clinical Nutrition* in 2009. She also indicated that regular nut consumption "probably" reduces the risk of diabetes mellitus among women and protects against gallstone disease in both men and women (Sabaté and Ang, "Nuts and Health Outcomes," 1643s).

NUTS

People who eat nuts regularly have a much lower risk of dying from heart disease. This may in part be due to the vitamin E in nuts, which is thought to keep LDL cholesterol from oxidizing and becoming dangerous to heart health. Nuts also contain an amino acid that may convert to nitric oxide, a substance known to help expand blood vessels. Nitric oxide also helps to keep the platelets in blood from sticking together, further decreasing the risk of heart disease (Yeager, *The Doctors Book of Food Remedies*, 446).

A Spanish study published in the *Archives of Internal Medicine* in 2008 found that participants in a Mediterranean diet that included regular consumption of nuts experienced reversion of metabolic syndrome at a much higher rate than those participants in a control group (Salas-Salvadó and others, "Effect of a Mediterranean Diet"). Metabolic syndrome is a set of symptoms that place an individual at increased risk for type 2 diabetes, coronary artery disease, and stroke. The symptoms are carrying extra weight around one's middle, high blood pressure, high triglycerides, insulin resistance, and low HDL (good) cholesterol. I feel it's important to mention here that in addition to consuming the right foods, daily exercise is highly recommended for keeping these symptoms in check.

Nuts also supply protein and usually provide "good fats." Because of their high fat content they are a very satisfying snack and are readily substituted for meat as a source of protein. Among nuts, peanuts (actually a legume) have the most protein. Ounce per ounce, peanuts provide more protein than one would get from fish or beef. Peanuts also provide a complete protein that has all the essential amino acids our bodies require. Tree nuts, such as walnuts, cashews, and almonds have the highest amounts of omega-3 fatty acids, which we know are critical for brain health, both intellectually and emotionally, as well as for heart health (Yeager, *The Doctors Book of Food Remedies,* 447, 446).

Nuts are a good source of fiber and vitamin E, which have both been associated with reduced risk for certain cancers. Research at Purdue University demonstrated that a substance in the vitamin E from walnuts and pecans killed prostate- and lung-cancer cells in the laboratory without harming healthy cells (Yeager, *The Doctors Book of Food Remedies*, 447).

Despite the high fat and calorie content of nuts, long-term nut eaters have been shown to have lower body weight (Sabaté and Ang, "Nuts and Health Outcomes," 1643s). You need to eat only a handful (about 1 ounce) per day to derive the health benefits of nuts.

Australian researchers are finding that—in addition to positive influences of nuts on heart disease, diabetes, cancer, gallstones, and obesity—the consumption of nuts reduces the risk of age-related macular degeneration, the leading cause of blindness in people over the age of sixty-five. In her longitudinal study, Jennifer Tan found that participants who ate one serving of fish per week had a 31 percent lower risk of developing macular degeneration and that those who ate one to two servings of nuts per week had a 35 percent lower risk of the same (Tan and others, "Dietary Fatty Acids").

HERBS AND SPICES

In the typical American diet, we are unaccustomed to eating many spices. It is a rare household that doesn't have salt and pepper shakers on the kitchen table, and they provide most of the seasoning we use. In Greek cooking we enjoy herbs and spices on a daily basis, and they have many health benefits. Garlic and oregano are two that are used extensively.

As I mentioned earlier, garlic is known to thin the blood, lower blood pressure, lower cholesterol, improve immunity, decrease chronic inflammation, and fight microbes. There is some evidence that suggests it may protect against cancer as well. Oregano provides antibacterial, antifungal, antiviral, and antiparasitic protection. Ginger is an antioxidant, aids digestion, and reduces inflammation. Rosemary also reduces inflammation as well as promoting detoxification. Widely used in traditional Greek desserts, cinnamon has antifungal properties and is effective in controlling diabetes and in lowering LDL while raising HDL cholesterol (Hyman and Liponis, *Ultraprevention*, 278–79; Yeager, *The Doctors Book of Food Remedies*, 587). And cloves contain two powerful antioxidants that prevent free radicals, thereby protecting healthy cells and preventing damaging oxidation (Yeager, *The Doctors Book of Food Remedies*, 586).

Other spices seem to be able to arrest harmful substances in the body. For example aflatoxin, a mold that can cause liver cancer, can be rendered ineffective by nutmeg, ginger, cumin, black pepper, and coriander (Yeager, *The Doctors Book of Food Remedies*, 586).

GREEK DESSERTS

The consideration of the health benefits of nuts and spices is the perfect lead-in to this dessert chapter because traditional Greek desserts use a variety of nuts and spices, which provide a tasty infusion of nutrients into many recipes. Adding nuts and spices to cereals, yogurt, salads, and grains presents a great opportunity to add flavor and nutrients—with a whole host of health benefits—to any meal.

FROM BANANA TIRES TO "WHO MADE THE *BAKLAVA*?"

I wasn't always a cook. I got my start in middle school in home-ec class. Mostly I loved baking. I had a molar of a sweet tooth. I did quite well by following recipes—except for the time I doubled the cherry cobbler recipe when making it for my family and doubled the baking soda along with all the other ingredients. It was pretty salty, but my dad was a great sport when it came to desserts, and I remember that his praise relieved my own disappointment.

Anyway, by the time I met Harris, I was a pretty decent baker, though perhaps overconfident. One day I noticed he had a bunch of overripe bananas, and I knew he was expecting a friend for the weekend, so I volunteered to make banana bread. Thinking I could do it without a recipe, I casually started adding ingredients. He didn't have a loaf pan, but I discovered two round cake pans, so I used those. The breads smelled great as they baked, but when we cut into them they were flat-out rubbery. Dick, Harris's friend, coined them "banana tires," and I've yet to live it down (though of late he has e-mailed me for soup recipes).

The good news is I'm continuing to improve. Several years ago, when we were new to South Carolina, I managed the county health department. As is typically the case in the world of public health, there is rarely enough time or money to meet all the needs. I oversaw twelve program areas with two-hundred staff, and when the holidays came, there was no money for bonuses, turkeys, or anything but a handshake and a "thank-you." So I baked.

I had the idea to make *baklava* because it was uncommon and rather "exotic." I made thirteen large trays of *baklava,* one for each program and one for the administration. Though Harris complained I was putting him in the poorhouse by purchasing pounds and pounds of walnuts, I got pretty good at making it, and folks really seemed to like it.

With all that experience I didn't hesitate to volunteer when I heard from our friend Tina, a Ph.D. candidate, that the Greek students were cooking for an international festival: "I'll make the *baklava!*"

Well it turned out that the would-be harshest judges, the Greek students themselves, loved my *baklava*. Tina reported that everyone who tasted it asked, "Who made the *baklava?*" And the standard reply was, "Dr. Pastides' wife, and she's not even Greek!"

The following year the students asked for the recipe so they could make many trays for the festival. I was more than flattered to share it; it's the same as the one on page 180. Make it, and impress your family and friends. It's easy to follow the recipe, and it's pretty tough to make *baklava* tires.

Anise and Sesame Cookies—
Koulourakia

Koulouri (to use the singular) is a delicious cookie often served in Cyprus with coffee in the afternoon. It's commonly found rolled in sesame seeds. Since anise seeds were readily available in the market in Larnaca and because I love the mildly licorice flavor, I decided to try anise seeds in this recipe. It's been a big hit. I have to be certain to make extra when serving *koulourakia* to my *parea* (group of friends) because they all like to take at least one "to go" for the next morning.

PREHEAT THE OVEN to 375 degrees.

Cream butter and sugar in a mixer until smooth and fluffy. Blend in the beaten eggs.

Warm the milk over medium heat, but do not boil it. In a separate, small mixing bowl, stir the baking soda and baking powder into the warm milk until the powder and soda dissolve. The mixture will foam and expand in volume.

Gently blend this milk mixture into the butter-sugar mixture. Stir in ½ teaspoon of anise seeds and then gradually blend in the sifted flour. The dough should pull away from the sides of the bowl.

Chill the cookie dough in the refrigerator for a minimum of 15 minutes before beginning to shape it. When the dough is chilled, pat your hands with some of the remaining ¼ cup of flour before quickly rolling a heaping tablespoon of dough into a 5-inch log. Then roll the log in a blend of ¼ cup anise seeds and ¼ cup sesame seeds. Shape the log into a circle, overlapping the ends.

Grease your cookie sheets and place the cookies 2 inches apart. Brush the tops with milk. Bake the *koulourakia* until the cookies are light brown, approximately 15 minutes.

Makes 2 dozen large cookies

⅔ cup (10 ⅔ tablespoons) unsalted butter
1 cup sugar
2 eggs, well beaten
⅓ cup milk (nonfat works fine)
½ teaspoon baking soda
2 teaspoons baking powder
½ teaspoon anise seeds
3 cups unbleached flour, sifted

¼ cup unbleached flour
¼ cup anise seeds
¼ cup sesame seeds

Canola-oil spray for greasing cookie sheet

¼ cup milk for brushing cookie tops

The colder the dough, the easier it will be to roll out the cookies, so it is not a problem to leave it in the refrigerator for a longer period of time.

Walnut and Filo Pastry— *Baklava*

If I could characterize this *baklava,* I would say that it's not too sweet, too dry, or too wet. In each bite it offers a nice mouthful of nuts that are not too finely ground. Others have said some *baklava* has so many layers of filo dough that they find it tough. Over the years I've learned to cut back on the filo dough, using just enough to hold the nuts inside.

For a variation of *baklava* substitute almonds, pecans, or pistachio nuts. All are delicious!

Making the *baklava*:

1 pound walnut halves

⅓ cup brown sugar

2 teaspoons cinnamon

6 tablespoons butter

½ pound prepared, frozen filo, thawed in refrigerator for 24 hours before using

¼ cup milk

20 whole cloves

PREHEAT THE OVEN to 350 degrees.

Place the walnuts in a food processor and process in short intervals until the walnuts are in small pieces but not ground into "flour." In a medium-size bowl, mix the nuts with the brown sugar and cinnamon. Set this mixture aside.

Melt the butter and brush the bottom of a 9 x 13-inch baking pan. Layer 6 sheets of filo, placing them lengthwise and buttering after each one. Then place 2 sheets across the width of the pan, letting the dough hang over the edges. Brush each sheet with butter. Put half the nut mixture on top of the filo and spread it evenly. Turn the overhanging edges of filo in on top of the nuts and butter these edges. Then place 1 sheet of filo over the nuts lengthwise and butter. Next place 2 more sheets of filo across the width, letting edges dangle over. Brush with butter, then top with remaining nuts. Spread the nuts evenly, fold in the overhanging filo, and brush with butter. Finish by topping with the remaining sheets of filo, one at a time, brushing each sheet with melted butter. Using the brush, press all the edges down into the pan and butter the edges well.

Using a sharp knife, carefully cut the baklava into 20 pieces, cutting all the way through to the pan. Stick a whole clove into the center of each piece; these provide flavor and hold the layers of filo in place.

Finally brush the cut edges of the pieces of *baklava* with milk to prevent them from curling up while baking.

Bake uncovered in a 350-degree oven for approximately 30 minutes or until the *baklava* is a deep golden brown.

While the *baklava* is baking, make the syrup.

Mix the brown sugar, water, maple syrup, lemon juice, lemon peel, cloves, and cinnamon sticks in a saucepan. Bring to a boil over medium-high heat, cover the pan, lower the temperature, and simmer for 5 minutes. Remove the lid and simmer, stirring, for another couple of minutes. The syrup will thicken slightly. Remove the pan from the heat, add the rose water and honey, and mix well. Let the syrup cool.

When the *baklava* is fully baked, remove it from the oven and pour the cooled syrup over the hot *baklava.* Allow the *baklava* to cool and absorb the syrup before serving.

If you wish to serve the *baklava* on the same day you make it, prepare it several hours in advance to allow time for the syrup to be completely absorbed.

Baklava can be made a day or two before serving. After it cools, cover the pan with aluminum foil and store it in the refrigerator. *Baklava* should not be served chilled, so take it out of the refrigerator several hours before serving to bring it to room temperature.

Serves 20 happy people!

Making the *baklava* syrup:

1 cup brown sugar
$\frac{1}{2}$ cup water
$\frac{1}{4}$ cup real maple syrup
1 tablespoon fresh lemon juice
2 small strips lemon peel
6–8 whole cloves
2 cinnamon sticks (2–3 inch pieces)
$\frac{1}{4}$ teaspoon rose water
$\frac{1}{2}$ cup honey

Cinnamon Cookies with Syrup and Walnuts—*Finikia*

Sweeter than *koulourakia, finikia* may still be classified as "adult" cookies. They are wonderful served for dessert with ice cream or rice pudding, but they are also enjoyed just by themselves with coffee or tea. *Finikia* are dipped into a syrup similar to that of *baklava,* but they do not rest in the syrup. One dips the warm cookies into the syrup and removes them quickly. With this method the cookies are sweetened and flavored by the syrup, but they don't soak it up, which would make them too wet and soggy.

Some *finikia* recipes call for a lot more sugar in the cookie dough than this one. I don't think the extra sugar is needed because the syrup nicely sweetens the cookies and allows one to appreciate the cinnamon and clove flavoring.

PREHEAT THE OVEN to 280 degrees.

Mix the sugar, orange juice, melted butter, brandy, cinnamon, sea salt, and baking powder to combine. Gradually stir in the flour. The glossy dough will pull away from the sides of the bowl as you stir it. Knead it a bit to combine well.

Using about a tablespoon of dough, shape it into an oval and place it on an ungreased cookie sheet. When the sheet is full of cookies, placed about 2 inches apart, bake for approximately 30 minutes until the bottoms are a light-golden brown.

While the cookies are baking, prepare the syrup.

Mix all the syrup ingredients in a saucepan and cook over medium-high heat, stirring until the syrup comes to a rolling boil. Stir for one minute and then remove from the heat.

Grind the walnuts finely in a food processor.

When the *finikia* are baked, place the warm cookies in the syrup one at a time. Turn each cookie once so it gets coated, and then remove it from the syrup.

Dip the top of each moistened cookie into the ground walnuts and place the cookie on a rack to let excess syrup drain. Repeat for all cookies.

Place *finikia* on a serving dish or store in a cookie tin rather than in a plastic container.

Makes 3 dozen cookies

Cookie dough:

½ cup sugar

½ cup orange juice

1 cup butter, melted

¼ cup brandy

2 teaspoons ground cinnamon

1 teaspoon sea salt

2 teaspoons baking powder

3½ cups unbleached flour

Syrup:

¾ cup sugar

½ cup honey

¾ cup water

2 cinnamon sticks

10 whole cloves

1 cup shelled walnuts

Spiced Berry Soup

2 cups fresh strawberries

2 cups fresh raspberries

1 tablespoon brown sugar

$\frac{1}{8}$ teaspoon ground cardamom

$\frac{1}{4}$ teaspoon ground ginger

$\frac{1}{2}$ teaspoon ground cinnamon

1 cup orange juice

$1\frac{1}{2}$ cups grape juice

WASH THE BERRIES and strain off excess water.

Puree 1½ cups of the strawberries and 1½ cups of the raspberries in a food processor with the brown sugar, cardamom, ginger, and cinnamon.

Transfer the puree to a medium-size pot and add the orange juice and grape juice. Start cooking the Spiced Berry Soup over medium-high heat, stirring until the soup just begins to boil. Then lower the heat and simmer while stirring for about 3–5 minutes to blend the flavors and reduce the contents slightly. Remove the pot from the heat, pour the soup through a fine mesh sieve into a bowl, and refrigerate the soup so it is well chilled before serving.

Slice the remaining strawberries and add them and the whole raspberries to the chilled soup.

Serve Spiced Berry Soup with a small scoop of Honey Frozen Yogurt (page 185).

Serves 8

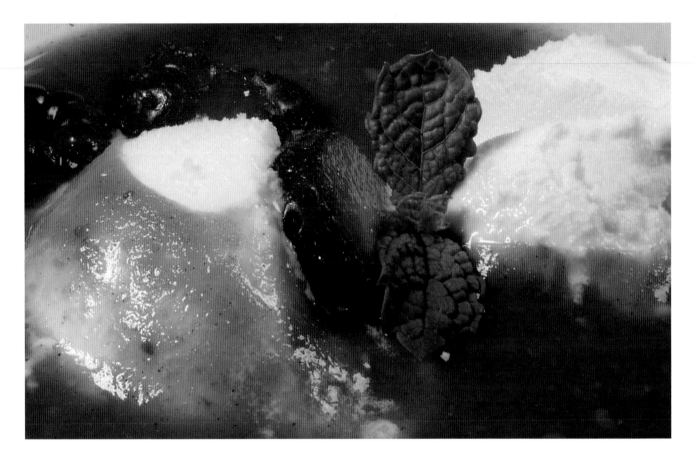

Honey Frozen Yogurt

IN A LARGE BOWL, stir together the yogurt, honey, and buttermilk until all the ingredients are well blended and smooth. Chill the mixture in the refrigerator until it is very cold and then transfer it to an ice-cream maker. Process until the mixture thickens, approximately 25–30 minutes. Transfer the yogurt mixture to a flat airtight container and freeze to firm.

Five to ten minutes before serving, take the Honey Frozen Yogurt from the freezer and let it sit on the counter to soften a bit.

Serves 8

2 cups plain Greek-style thick yogurt (nonfat works fine)
¾ cup honey
½ cup buttermilk (skim or low fat works well)

Rose-Scented Custard Pie—
Galaktoboureko

For the custard filling:

4 cups milk (2 percent)

¼ cup sugar

½ cup semolina (farina)

1 tablespoon butter

2 eggs at room temperature

1 teaspoon vanilla

½ cup butter, melted

18 sheets prepared, frozen filo, thawed in refrigerator for
24 before using

For the syrup:

1 cup water

1 cup sugar

2 tablespoons honey

2 cinnamon sticks

6–8 whole cloves

¾ teaspoon rose water

PREHEAT THE OVEN to 350 degrees.

Heat the milk in a heavy saucepan over medium-high heat until it is just beginning to boil. Add ¼ cup sugar, the semolina, and the butter. Reduce the heat to medium and cook while stirring until the custard is thickened enough to coat a wooden spoon, about 5–7 minutes. Test by running your finger across a wooden coated spoon to create a "path" through the custard. If the path stays clear, the custard is ready. Remove the pan from the heat.

Beat the eggs and add 5 tablespoons of hot milk, one at a time, stirring after each addition to raise the temperature of the eggs. Then whisk the eggs into the milk mixture. Add 1 teaspoon of vanilla and stir. Set aside.

Prepare a 9 X 13-inch baking pan by buttering the bottom and lining it with 9 sheets of filo dough, assuring that the bottom of the pan is completely covered and that the filo comes up the sides of the pan. That way the filo will surround the custard filling. Pour in the custard filling, and carefully bring the sides of filo over it. Top with the remaining sheets of filo, buttering each with a light touch so it won't tear. Tuck in all edges with the buttered brush.

Place the *galaktoboureko* in the oven and cook it for about 10–15 minutes, until the top sheets of filo begin to dry. Remove it from the oven and use a sharp knife to score the upper sheets of filo to mark pieces, being careful not to cut through the custard layer. Return it to the oven and bake for about another 35 minutes until the pie is golden brown on top and the custard is firm.

While the *galaktoboureko* is baking, make the syrup by combining 1 cup water, 1 cup sugar, 2 tablespoons of honey, 2 cinnamon sticks, and 6–8 whole cloves in a small saucepan. Bring the syrup to a boil over high heat. Stir, reduce the heat, and simmer until slightly thickened, about 15 minutes.

Remove the syrup from the heat and ¾ teaspoon of rose water. Remove the cinnamon sticks and cloves and let the syrup cool.

When the *galaktoboureko* is golden brown, remove it from the oven, and pour the cooled syrup over it.

Let the *galaktoboureko* stand until it is completely cooled before serving. This is best if you can let it stand for a few hours so the syrup can be absorbed.

Serves 16

Greek Wedding Cookies with Almonds—*Kourabiedes*

PREHEAT THE OVEN to 325 degrees.

Sift flour with baking powder and set aside.

In an electric mixer, cream melted butter with ¼ cup of confectioners' sugar. Then add the beaten egg yolk, brandy, and almond extract. Beat well.

Add the flour and baking-powder mixture ½ cup at a time until the batter is well blended.

Finely grind the blanched almonds in a food processor and fold them into the batter.

Shape 1 heaping tablespoon of dough into a crescent or oval shape and place it on an ungreased cookie sheet. As you shape the cookies, place them on the cookie sheet approximately 1 inch apart.

Bake for 25–30 minutes, until the cookies are firm. Do not overbake them. The bottoms of the cookies should be only slightly brown.

Cool the cookies and dust them with confectioners' sugar.

Makes approximately 2½ dozen *kourabiedes*

2½ cups unbleached flour
½ teaspoon baking powder
1 cup unsalted butter, melted
¼ cup confectioners' sugar
1 egg yolk, beaten
2 tablespoons brandy
1 teaspoon almond extract
½ cup blanched almonds

1 cup confectioners' sugar
for dusting cookies

Rice Pudding with Raisins and Cinnamon—*Rizogalo*

¾ cup white rice (long-grain Basmati)

6 cups milk (2 percent)

¼ cup sugar

¼ teaspoon nutmeg

⅛ teaspoon sea salt

2 egg yolks

1 teaspoon vanilla extract

½ cup raisins

Cinnamon to sprinkle

Most recipes recommend short-grain rice for pudding, but I find the results too gummy for my taste.

If you are not fond of raisins in your rice pudding, leave them out and increase the sugar to ½ cup.

COMBINE THE RAW RICE, milk, sugar, nutmeg, and sea salt in a heavy pan. Bring to a boil over high heat, cover, and reduce the heat to low. Simmer until the rice is tender, approximately 20 minutes.

Beat the egg yolks in a small bowl and gradually add 4–5 spoonfuls of the rice mixture, one at a time, to bring up the yolk temperature. Pour the yolk mixture into the pan and continue cooking over medium heat, while stirring, for about 20 minutes. The pudding should have thickened enough to coat the back of the spoon. At this point the mixture is still somewhat liquidy. The rice pudding will firm up as it cools, so don't overcook it.

Remove the pan from the heat and stir in the vanilla extract and the raisins. Stir to combine and cool the pudding to room temperature before serving it. Top it with a sprinkle of cinnamon.

Serves 6

Greek Apple Tart with Walnut-Crumb Topping— *Milopita*

This is a foolproof recipe, as the crust is not rolled out. Fill it with any fruit for a delicious dessert that will earn rave reviews.

Tart crust:

2 cups unbleached flour

¼ teaspoon sea salt

½ cup sugar

1½ teaspoon baking powder

½ cup unsalted cold butter

2 egg yolks

Filling:

6 tart apples, peeled, cored, and thinly sliced

¼ cup sugar

1 tablespoon lemon juice

1 teaspoon cinnamon

¼ cup water

McIntosh apples work well because they are juicy.

PREHEAT THE OVEN to 375 degrees.

Combine the flour, sea salt, sugar and baking powder in a food processor. Cut the cold butter into pieces, add it to the food processor, and pulse to combine. Add the egg yolks and process well. The mixture will look like coarse bread crumbs. Reserve one cup of tart-crust mixture for the topping. Press the remaining crust mixture into the bottom and up the sides of a 9 x 11-inch baking pan.

Combine the sliced apples, ¼ cup sugar, lemon juice, cinnamon, and water in a saucepan, cover and cook over medium-high heat for 15 minutes, stirring occasionally. Apples should be half-soft, and there should be some liquid in the saucepan. Using a slotted spoon place the apples on the dough in the baking pan. Reserve the liquid (apple syrup) for the topping.

To the reserved tart-crust mixture, add the lemon peel and chopped walnuts and mix well. Sprinkle this mixture over the apples. Melt the butter in the saucepan with the apple syrup. Drizzle the *milopita* with the butter-apple syrup and bake in the middle of a preheated oven for 40–45 minutes, until the top is golden brown.

Serves 12

Topping:

1 cup tart-crust mixture

½ teaspoon grated lemon peel

½ cup finely chopped walnuts

2 tablespoons butter

Reserved apple syrup

Spiced Walnut Cake— *Karidopita*

PREHEAT THE OVEN to 350 degrees.

Prepare a 9-inch round cake pan by greasing and flouring the bottom and sides.

In a small bowl, sift together the flour, sea salt, cinnamon, ground cloves, and baking powder. Set this mixture aside.

In an electric mixer, beat the egg whites until foamy and gradually beat in the sugar. Continue beating until the egg whites are stiff and glossy white. Beat the four egg yolks with a whisk and then fold them into the egg whites. Next fold in the flour mixture.

In a food processor, chop the walnuts until they are as finely ground as possible. Fold the walnuts into the batter.

Pour the batter into the prepared cake pan and bake the cake in the center of the preheated oven for approximately 35 minutes or until a tester comes out clean.

While the cake is baking, combine the honey, water, and cinnamon sticks and cook over high heat until boiling. Lower the heat to simmer and let the syrup simmer for about ten minutes, stirring occasionally.

Remove the syrup from the heat and let it cool.

When your *karidopita* is baked, let it cool slightly (for at least 10 minutes) and turn it out of the pan. When serving slices, reheat the syrup and drizzle some on each slice.

Serves 8

Canola oil spray
Flour to prepare pan
1 cup unbleached flour
$\frac{1}{2}$ teaspoon sea salt
$\frac{1}{2}$ teaspoon cinnamon
$\frac{1}{2}$ teaspoon ground cloves
2 teaspoons baking powder

6 egg whites
1 cup sugar
4 egg yolks
1 pound shelled walnuts

Syrup:

$\frac{1}{2}$ cup honey
1 cup water
2 cinnamon sticks

Pistachio and Honey Coffee Cake

½ cup butter, softened

1 cup sugar

2 eggs

1 teaspoon baking soda

1½ teaspoons baking powder

1 cup strained plain yogurt,
   or Greek-style thick yogurt

1 teaspoon almond extract

¼ teaspoon sea salt

2 cups unbleached flour

Butter for preparing pan

Nut mixture:

1 cup shelled pistachio nuts

⅓ cup sesame seeds

⅓ cup honey

1 teaspoon cinnamon

PREHEAT THE OVEN to 350 degrees.

In an electric mixer, cream the softened butter and the sugar thoroughly. Add the eggs one at a time, beating thoroughly after each addition.

Dissolve the baking soda and baking powder in the yogurt. Stir well to dissolve. The yogurt will fluff up. Add the almond extract. Set this mixture aside.

Sift the sea salt and flour together and add it to the creamed mixture alternately with the strained yogurt. Mix well.

Butter a 9-inch round baking pan. Pour the batter into the pan.

Make the nut mixture by finely chopping the pistachios in the food processor. In a small bowl, combine them with the sesame seeds, honey, and cinnamon. Mix well. Drop the honey-nut mixture by spoonfuls on top of the cake batter.

Bake for approximately 45 minutes, until a cake tester comes out clean when inserted into the center of the cake. Cover the cake with aluminum foil or parchment paper for the final 20 minutes so the honey-nut mixture doesn't burn.

Serves 8

Yogurt Parfaits with Blueberries and Lemon Curd

If you are looking for a dessert with a taste that belies how easy it is to make, you need to try this one. It's a winner every time! But remember, the best time to make this is when you can get local blueberries. The reason people adore the simple tomato salad in Greece is because the tomatoes are ripened on their vines and picked just before they are eaten. There are no blueberries as good as those you pick yourself or buy locally in season.

1 quart plain yogurt (nonfat tastes fine)

4–6 teaspoons lemon curd

1 pint fresh blueberries, washed

8–12 small mint leaves for garnish

PREPARE THE YOGURT by straining it through a cheesecloth or fine mesh strainer for 20–30 minutes in your refrigerator. Discard the liquid that results.

Spoon about ½ cup of the strained yogurt into a parfait glass. Top with a scant teaspoon of lemon curd (recipe on facing page) and divide the blueberries equally, sprinkling them into each parfait glass. Top with mint leaves to garnish.

Serves 4–6

Tangiest Lemony Lemon Curd

Yogurt Parfaits with Blueberries and Lemon Curd are greatly enhanced by homemade lemon curd. My friend Elaine's sister grows lemons, which Elaine uses to make what I've dubbed "The Tangiest Lemony Lemon Curd." Here is her recipe.

MELT THE BUTTER in a small, heavy saucepan over medium-low heat.

Remove the pan from the heat and whisk in the sugar, lemon juice, lemon zest, egg yolks and sea salt. Whisk until smooth.

Cook the mixture, whisking constantly, until it thickens enough to coat a wooden spoon, approximately 7–10 minutes. (To test, coat the spoon with the lemon curd and run your finger through the coating. If the path your finger creates stays, the curd is done.) Do not allow the lemon curd to boil.

Immediately pour the lemon curd through a strainer into a bowl. Let it cool to room temperature, whisking occasionally. Transfer the lemon curd to a covered jar and refrigerate. Stored this way, the lemon curd will keep in the refrigerator for about a month or in the freezer for three months.

Makes about 1½ cups.

½ cup unsalted butter
¾ cup sugar
½ cup fresh lemon juice,
    strained of seeds and pulp
3 tablespoons finely grated
    lemon zest
7 extra-large egg yolks,
    slightly beaten
pinch of sea salt

Militsa's Homemade Lemonade,
p. 206

9. BEVERAGES

■

Militsa's Homemade Lemonade
Chamomile Tea
Sour Cherry Soda—*Vissinada*

*The ancient Greek use of "nectar" to indicate wine
is itself a good example of the relationship between
wine and prevention of disease. The Greek etymology
of the word nectar means "to escape from death."*

Dipak Das and Fulvio Ursini, eds.,
Alcohol and Wine in Health and Disease

DRINKING IN MODERATION has been proven to be heart healthy. In fact it is better than being a teetotaler for people without contraindications to alcohol consumption. According to Arthur Klatsky: "'Heavy steady drinkers' had the highest mortality; 'abstainers' were next; and 'moderate drinkers' had the lowest mortality" (Klatsky, "Alcohol and Cardiovascular Disease," 8).

STUDYING ALCOHOL AND HEALTH

A number of epidemiological studies conducted in various countries have consistently shown a decrease of 30 percent in the risk of coronary heart disease among moderate drinkers; that is, those who consume 10–40 grams per day, which is roughly one to three drinks per day (Klatsky, foreword).

Klatsky based his definition of "heavy" drinking on what the bulk of epidemiological studies has shown to be the level of drinking above which harm is usually seen, so drinking three drinks or more per day would classify someone as a "heavy" drinker, whereas fewer than three drinks a day was termed "moderate." A study published in the *British Medical Journal* in 1997 sought to ascertain how much alcohol and what frequency of consumption would yield the greatest benefit. The study determined that the men who had the lowest risk for a major coronary event reported consuming one to three drinks per day over five to six days per week. The women who reported one or two drinks daily over five to six days per week were considered at lowest risk (McElduff and Dobson, "How Much Alcohol and How Often?").

Dr. Walt Willett reported that moderate alcohol consumption protects against heart disease and ischemic strokes by "raising levels of HDL, the protective form of cholesterol, and reducing the formation of clots that can block arteries in the heart, neck and brain" (Willett, *Eat, Drink, and Be Healthy*, 154). "The Effects of Moderate Alcohol Consumption on Cognitive Function in Women," published in the *New England Journal of Medicine*, reported that women who drank one drink per day had better mean cognitive scores than nondrinkers. The researchers concluded that their data suggested one drink per day does not impair cognitive function and may actually decrease the risk of cognitive decline (Stampler and others, "Effects of Moderate Alcohol Consumption").

Concern about recommending the consumption of alcoholic beverages is warranted, however, as alcohol contributes to preventable deaths and injuries and is often a factor in the demise of interpersonal relationships. Clearly individuals with a history of alcoholism in their families or with alcohol-abuse issues should not be advised to drink alcoholic beverages. And while some studies have shown a benefit to cognitive abilities among moderate drinkers, we also have evidence that too much alcohol can leach the beneficial omega-3 fatty acids from the brain (Simopoulos and Robinson, *The Omega Diet,* 40).

A serious concern emerged when the Nurses' Health Study reported that drinking two drinks per day increased the chances of developing breast cancer by 20 to 25 percent. Further studies have shown that the risk associated with breast cancer and alcohol consumption in women is seen mostly in women who do not get enough folic acid in their diets (Willett, *Eat, Drink, and Be Healthy,* 154–55). Avoiding breast cancer is another good reason to follow a traditional Greek diet.

RED WINE

Current studies bode well for choosing red wine as the spirit of choice. If as part of a lifestyle change, we seek out locally grown organic vegetables because we appreciate the taste and value the nutrients, and if we purchase the meat of free-range animals because it is leaner and has the highest concentration of omega-3 fatty acids, then it follows that we would choose red wine over other alcoholic beverages for its phenols. White wines do not offer nearly the phenolic content of reds. The total amount of phenols found in a glass of red wine is approximately 200 mg. By comparison there are only about 40 mg of phenols in a glass of white wine.

White wines are made by quickly pressing the juice away from the grape solids. To make red wines, the juice is fermented with the skin and seeds. The grape skin and seeds contain most of the phenols. Red wine is a "whole berry extract" and white wine a "juice product" (Waterhouse, "Wine Phenolics," 21).

Red wine can prevent heart disease and stroke and control intestinal bacteria. While the alcohol in red wine raises HDLs, its polyphenols, such as quercetin and resveratrol, prevent the LDLs from oxidizing and in that way discourage blood clots. Researchers have also found that wine is effective against intestinal bacteria such as shigella, salmonella, and E coli (Yeager, *The Doctors Book of Food Remedies,* 663–65).

A report published in May 2008 cited a study from the University of California, San Diego, School of Medicine suggesting that a glass of red wine a day could provide protection for the liver. Nonalcoholic fatty liver disease (NAFLD) is the most common liver disease in the United States and is expected to increase along with rising obesity. In their study the researchers found that those participants who drank a glass of red wine per day had half the risk of NAFLD ("Red Wine Keeps Liver Healthy"). Since this effect was not apparent for beer or hard liquor drinkers, it is thought that the polyphenols may be providing the benefit.

As more research is conducted into the phytonutrients of red wine, more light will be shed on its health benefits. Researchers at the University of South Carolina are finding that mice fed a diet including large doses of resveratrol are living two and a half times their usual life expectancies.

As long as individuals can limit intake to one glass per day for women and two glasses for men, there are many benefits, and we hope that a longer healthy life is the primary one.

TELL ME NURSES LIE

I'm not wild about cocktails. Unless I'm in Mexico, you won't find me ordering a margarita. I do like a Guinness occasionally, especially on St. Patty's Day. But I love wine. I once described myself to my internist as a "macrobiotic wino." I'm no longer macrobiotic, and I'm trying not to be a wino! I enjoy wine most with food. And here's the thing: I like to have just enough wine to end exactly when my meal ends.

I learned years ago that during a multiple-course dinner, where one is likely to drink different wines, it is advisable to drink a glass of water for every glass of wine one consumes. That's a great way to prevent the more immediate ill effects from the wine, such as waking and bolting upright in bed at 2:00 A.M. from all that metabolized sugar.

But I was devastated when the news from the Nurses' Health Study confirmed suspicions that drinking more than one glass of wine per day was associated with an increased risk for breast cancer. Being married to an epidemiologist, I've taken many opportunities to question his colleagues about the association between alcohol and breast cancer. Most have told me to stick to one glass of wine per day. The most lenient interpretation I ever got from one of them was the suggestion that I stop at one and a half glasses per day.

So I read lots of abstracts of studies looking at this association. Most seem to bear out the findings. My final hope is that when asked how much they drink, the nurses in the health study lied, underreporting the amount they actually consumed. In the meantime I've cut back on wine and increased my consumption of vegetables.

The relationship we Americans have with alcohol is at least as dysfunctional as our relationship with food. When I was in college I wanted to be an alcoholism counselor. I was talked out of it by my preceptor at an internship in a program for alcoholics. Fortunately he guided me to a degree in public-health administration, where I could run a program for alcoholics if I chose to but would not be limited to that alone. During that internship I learned that we drink as a social lubricant. We drink when our team wins. We drink when our team loses. And we drink when the game gets rained out. The first sips make us feel better, and we think that the more we drink the better we'll feel—until the next morning. The next morning, with pounding heads and queasy stomachs, we swear off alcohol entirely, at least until that evening when company's coming for dinner or our team is on television.

I'm not saying that people in other countries abstain, but I have noticed during many trips to Greece that people there drink wine from very small glasses. Just as our dinner plates have expanded from seven to twelve inches so have our wine glasses. Realize that the studies on wine consumption are talking about a five-ounce glass, not ten or twelve ounces, the size some wine glasses have grown to.

Greeks typically drink during a meal, not generally before or after a meal. As in other areas of the Mediterranean, Greeks mainly drink wine. There is ouzo, which is usually served to *xenos* (foreigners) for the entertainment of locals. During our sabbatical I was told my Greek language skills improved when I had an ouzo, but trust me, that's where the benefit ended. And there is brandy, which older men will occasionally have a glass of in the evening. But compared to Americans, who have made a recreational activity of sitting and drinking just to drink, Greeks don't drink much.

I love this quotation from the sixteenth-century German alchemist known as Paracelsus: "A food [or wine] can be also a drug or a poison, the difference is just a matter of dosage" (Gronbaek, "Type of Alcohol"). For those of you without drinking problems and without contraindications for consuming alcohol, may I offer another quote from a study published in the *British Medical Journal:* "A glass of wine with dinner every evening may be the best advice you can give them" (Gronbaek and others, "Influence of Sex, Age, Body Mass Index, and Smoking").

May I also offer you refreshing recipes for homemade lemonade, sour cherry soda, and chamomile tea. Στην υγειά σας (*Stin ygia sas*)—to your health!

Militsa's Homemade Lemonade

It's wonderful to visit a country where lemons are plentiful, large, and juicy. This recipe is from a dear family friend, Militsa, who lives in Nicosia, Cyprus. With Cypriot lemons, this lemonade is exquisite! A daily glass in the middle of the hot afternoons carried me through the summer.

With this recipe you make a concentrate, which you can keep in your refrigerator and mix up a glass whenever you'd like. It's also a great medicinal remedy for anyone starting a cold or scratchy throat. In that case I make it with boiling water as one would make tea. Hot lemonade is a sure cure for a budding cold.

I cup fresh-squeezed lemon juice

1 cup sugar

SQUEEZE THE JUICE from as many lemons as needed to derive one cup of lemon juice. Strain out any seeds.

Combine the lemon juice and sugar in a bowl with a pouring spout and whisk until the sugar dissolves.

Transfer this "lemonade concentrate" into a glass bottle with a screw top and store in the refrigerator.

To make a glass of lemonade, fill a tall glass with ice, shake the bottle of lemonade concentrate well, and pour approximately 2 inches of juice over the ice. Add cold water and lemon slices and stir.

Chamomile Tea

Greeks value chamomile for a number of medicinal purposes including relieving headaches, soothing puffy eyes, and calming stomach disorders or abdominal pain. Washing one's hair in chamomile tea is thought to make it shinier.

Chamomile has long been thought to promote sleep, calm the nerves, and prevent nightmares. Some studies have shown that chamomile has antiseptic properties, which are attributed to its polyphenols.

To make this mild-flavored tea, the dried chamomile flowers, leaves, and stems are crushed and steeped in boiling water for several minutes.

TO MAKE A CUP OF CHAMOMILE TEA, fill a tea ball with a heaping teaspoon of dried chamomile. Let the chamomile steep in one cup of boiling water for several minutes. Remove the tea ball and add honey if desired.

To make a pot of tea, use the same ratio of tea to water.

Enjoy chamomile tea hot.

1 heaping teaspoon dried chamomile
1 cup boiling water
Honey to taste (optional)

Sour Cherry Soda—*Vissinada*

Cherries are known to have vitamins A, E, and C as well as a host of antioxidants. Regular consumption of cherries is thought to relieve gout and arthritis symptoms in some people. Cherries are a healthy snack and make an excellent juice. *Vissinada* is a syrup made from sour cherries and sugar. It is diluted with water or sparkling water for a refreshing beverage.

The most difficult part of making *vissinada* is pitting all the cherries. If you love cherries, you might want to consider purchasing a cherry pitter, some of which can pit a pound of cherries in one minute!

PLACE THE PITTED SOUR CHERRIES in a food processor fitted with a steel blade and process until they are chopped but not pureed. Place the chopped cherries and juice in a bowl, cover, and refrigerate overnight.

Place a fine-mesh sieve over a bowl and spoon the chopped cherries and juice into the sieve. To extract the juice, press the cherries against the sieve using a clean hand.

Discard the solids, measure the extracted cherry juice and pour it into a saucepan. For every cup of cherry juice, add ¾ cup of granulated sugar to the saucepan.

Place the saucepan over medium heat and cook until the sugar dissolves. If sugar crystals form on the side of the pan, cover the pan for a few seconds, and they will dissolve.

Turn the heat up to medium high and add the lemon juice. Let the syrup boil uncovered for approximately 5 minutes. Do not stir. Adjust the heat if necessary, so the syrup continues to boil but does not boil over.

After five minutes the syrup should have thickened. Set it aside to cool. When it is fully cooled, decant it into a clean glass container with a tight-fitting lid. *Vissinada* should be stored in the refrigerator.

Drinks from *vissinada* may be made with flat or sparkling water. To make Sour Cherry Soda add 4–5 tablespoons of *vissinada* to a glass of sparkling water and ice. Stir to mix. A slice of lime or sprig of fresh mint is a lovely addition to this refreshing drink.

8 cups sour cherries, pitted
Approximately 2 cups granulated sugar
1 teaspoon lemon juice

REFERENCES

About.com:Cholesterol (accessed December 1, 2009).

Addrizzo, John R. "Use of Goat Milk and Goat Meat as Therapeutic Aids in Cardiovascular Disease." *Thyme for Goat,* online at http://thymeforgoat.com/Healthreport.shtml (accessed January 29, 2010).

Angelopoulos, P. D., H. J. Milionis, G. Moschonis, and Y. Manios. "Relations between Obesity and Hypertension: Preliminary Data from a Cross-Sectional Study in Primary Schoolchildren, the Children Study." *European Journal of Clinical Nutrition* 60 (May 17, 2006): 1226–34.

Benetou, V., A. Trichopoulou, P. Orfanos, A. Naska, P. Lagiou, P. Boffetta, and D. Trichopoulos. "Conformity to Traditional Mediterranean Diet and Cancer Incidence: The Greek Cohort." *British Journal of Cancer* 99 (July 1, 2008): 191–95.

Benjamin, Asher. *The Practical House Carpenter.* New York: Da Capo Press, 1972.

Campbell, T. Colin, with Thomas M. Campbell II. *The China Study: The Most Comprehensive Study of Nutrition Ever Conducted and the Startling Implications for Diet, Weight Loss and Long-Term Health.* Dallas: Benbella Books, 2005.

Chatzi, Leda, Gianna Apostolaki, Ioannis Bibakis, Isabel Skypala, Vasilki Bibaki-Liakou, Nikolaos Tzanakis, Manolis Kogevinas, and Paul Cullinan. "Protective Effects of Fruits, Vegetables, and the Mediterranean Diet on Asthma and Allergies among Children in Crete." *Thorax* 62 (August 2007): 677–83.

Chatzi, Leda, Matias Torrent, Isabelle Romieu, Raquel Garcia-Esteban, Carlos Ferrer, Jesus Vioque, Manolis Kogevinas, and Jordi Sunyer. "Mediterranean Diet in Pregnancy Is Protective for Wheeze and Atopy in Childhood." *Thorax* 63 (June 2008): 507–13.

Christianson, A., C. P. Howson, and B. Modell. *March of Dimes Global Report on Birth Defects: The Hidden Toll of Dying and Disabled Children.* White Plains, N.Y.: March of Dimes Birth Defects Foundation, 2006.

Das, Dipak, and Fulvio Ursini, eds. *Alcohol and Wine in Health and Disease.* Annals of the New York Academy of Science. New York: New York Academy of Science, 2002.

David, Elizabeth. *A Book of Mediterranean Food.* London: John Lehman, 1950. London: Cookery Book Club, 1968.

Edgar, Walter, ed. *The South Carolina Encyclopedia.* Columbia: University of South Carolina Press, 2006.

Estruch, R., M. A. Martínez-González, D. Corella, J. Salas-Salvadó, V. Ruiz-Gutiérrez, M. I. Covas, M. Fiol, E. Gómez-Gracia, M. C. López-Sabater, E. Vinyoles, F. Arós, M. Conde, C. Lahoz, J. Lapetra, G. Sáez, and E. Ros. "Effects of a Mediterranean-Style Diet on Cardiovascular Risk Factors: A Randomized Trial." *Annals of Internal Medicine* 145 (July 4, 2006): 1–11.

Garland, Sarah. *The Complete Book of Herbs and Spices.* New York: Viking, 1979.

Gronbaek, M., A. Deis, T. I. Sorensen, U. Becker, K. Borch-Johnsen, C. Muller, P. Schnohr, and G. Jensen. "Influence of Sex, Age, Body Mass Index, and Smoking on Alcohol Intake and Mortality." *British Medical Journal* 308 (January 29, 1994): 302–6.

Gronbaek, Morton. "Type of Alcohol and All-Cause and Coronary Heart Disease Mortality." In *Alcohol and Wine in Health and Disease,* edited by Dipak Das and Fulvio Ursini. Annals of the New York Academy of Science. New York: New York Academy of Science, 2002.

Guttersen, Connie. *The Sonoma Diet: Trimmer Waist, Better Health in Just 10 Days!* Des Moines: Meredith Books, 2005.

———. "Weighing in on Obesity." Online at www.calolive.org/nutritionists/findings (accessed December 7, 2006).

Heber, David, with Susan Bowerman. *What Color Is Your Diet?* New York: HarperCollins, 2001.

Heilmeyer, Marina. *Ancient Herbs.* Los Angeles: J. Paul Getty Museum, 2007.

Hyman, Mark, and Mark Liponis. *Ultraprevention: The Six-Week Plan That Will Make You Healthy for Life.* New York: Scribner, 2003.

Joseph, James A., Daniel Nadeau, and Anne Underwood. *The Color Code: A Revolutionary Eating Plan for Optimum Health.* New York: Philip Lief Group, 2002.

Klatsky, Arthur L. "Alcohol and Cardiovascular Disease: A Historical Overview." In *Alcohol and Wine in Health and Disease,* edited by Dipak Das and Fulvio Ursini, 7–15. Annals of the New York Academy of Science. New York: New York Academy of Science, 2002.

———. Foreword to *Alcohol and Wine in Health and Disease,* edited by Dipak Das and Fulvio Ursini, ix–x. Annals of the New York Academy of Science. New York: New York Academy of Science, 2002.

Klein, Maggie Blyth. *The Feast of the Olive: Cooking with Olives and Olive Oil.* San Francisco: Chronicle Books, 1994.

Knickerbocker, Peggy. *Olive Oil from Tree to Table.* San Francisco: Chronicle Books, 1997.

"Lentils." The World's Healthiest Foods (George Mateljan Foundation), online at http://www.whfoods.com/foodstoc.php (accessed December 1, 2009).

"Lima beans." The World's Healthiest Foods (George Mateljan Foundation), online at http://www.whfoods.com/foodstoc.php (accessed December 1, 2009).

McElduff, Patrick, and Annette Dobson. "How Much Alcohol and How Often? Population Based Case-Control Study of Alcohol Consumption and Risk of a Major Coronary Event." *British Medical Journal* 314 (April 19, 1997): 1159–64.

Mitrou, P. N., V. Kipnis, A. C. Thiébaut, J. Reedy, A. F. Subar, E. Wirfält, A. Flood, T. Mouw, A. R. Hollenbeck, M. F. Leitzmann, and A. Schatzkin. "Mediterranean Diet Pattern and Prediction of All-Cause Mortality in a U.S. Population: Results from the NIH-AARP Diet and Health Study." *Archives of Internal Medicine* 167 (December 10, 2007): 2461–68.

Nasca, A., E. Oikonomou, A. Trichopoulou, T. Psaltopoulou, and D. Trichopoulos. "Siesta in Healthy Adults and Coronary Mortality in the General Population." *Archives of Internal Medicine* 167 (February 12, 2007): 296–301.

"Red Wine Keeps Liver Healthy Suggests New Study by Lindsey Partose." Online at www.nutraingredients.com/news (accessed May 22, 2008).

Rosenthal, Elisabeth. "Fast Food Hits the Mediterranean: A Diet Succumbs." *New York Times,* September 24, 2008.

Sabaté, Joan, and Yen Ang. "Nuts and Health Outcomes: New Epidemiological Evidence." *American Journal of Clinical Nutrition* 89 (May 2009): 1643s–48s.

Salas-Salvadó, Jordi, et al. "Effect of a Mediterranean Diet Supplemented with Nuts on Metabolic Syndrome Status." *Archives of Internal Medicine* 168 (December 8/22, 2008): 2449–58.

Scarmeas, Nikolaos, Yaakov Stern, Richard Mayeux, Jennifer J. Manly, Nicole Schupf, and Jose A. Luchsinger. "Mediterranean Diet and Mild Cognitive Impairment." *Archives of Neurology* 66 (February 2009): 216–25.

Simopoulos, Artemis P., and Jo Robinson. *The Omega Diet: The Lifesaving Nutritional Program Based in the Diet of the Island of Crete.* New York: HarperPerennial, 1999.

Spiller, Gene A. *The Mediterranean Diets in Health and Disease.* New York: Van Nostrand Reinhold, 1991.

Stampler, Meir J., Jae Hee Kang, Jennifer Chen, Rebecca Cherry, and Francine Goldstein. "Effects of Moderate Alcohol Consumption on Cognitive Function in Women." *New England Journal of Medicine* 352 (January 20, 2005): 245–53.

Tan, Jennifer S. L., Jie Jin Wang, Victoria Flood, and Paul Mitchell. "Dietary Fatty Acids and the Ten-Year Incidence of Age Related Macular Degeneration." *Archives of Ophthalmology* 127 (May 2009): 656–65.

Trichopoulou, A., E. Vasilopoulou, K. Georga, S. Soukara, and V. Dilis. "Traditional Foods: Why and How to Sustain Them." *Trends in Food Science and Technology* 17 (September 2006): 498–504.

Waterhouse, Andrew L. "Wine Phenolics." In *Alcohol and Wine in Health and Disease,* edited by Dipak Das and Fulvio Ursini, 21–36. Annals of the New York Academy of Science. New York: New York Academy of Science, 2002.

Wilkins, John. *The Boastful Chef: The Discourse of Food in Ancient Greek Comedy.* Oxford & New York: Oxford University Press, 2000.

Willett, Walter C., with Patrick J. Skerrett. *Eat, Drink, and Be Healthy: The Harvard Medical School Guide to Healthy Eating.* New York: Free Press, 2005.

Yeager, Selene, and editors of *Prevention. The Doctors Book of Food Remedies.* Emmaus, Pa.: Rodale, 2007.

INDEX